Leading Organizational Change *Using* Action Learning

What Leaders Should Know Before Committing to a Consulting Contract

Leading Organizational Change *Using* Action Learning

What Leaders Should Know Before Committing to a Consulting Contract

Arthur M. Freedman
H. Skipton Leonard

Printed in the United States of America.

ISBN-13: 978-0615822556

ISBN-10: 061582255X

Ordering Information:
This book may be ordered through Amazon.com.

Published by:
Learning Thru Action, LLC
11354 Orchard Lane
Reston, VA 20190
www.learningthruaction.com
703.880.4915

Table of Contents

Acknowledgements

This book has truly been a global undertaking. We have gained many of our ideas and methods through our training and consulting around the world. Although it would be impossible to mention all of the colleagues, clients, and students who have influenced our thinking and made this book possible, we express special thanks to those with whom we have worked over the years in developing the techniques, methods and strategies that we employ in integrating the practices of action learning team coaching with organizational change and leadership development. We begin by recognizing our colleagues at the World Institute for Action Learning who, over the past seven years, have contributed to our thinking about training and practicing as action learning team coaches.

In particular, we recognize the small, diverse group of experienced thought and practice leaders in action learning with whom we launched the World Institute for Action Learning (WIAL) in 2006: Mike Marquardt, Peter Loan, Chuck Appleby, and Bea Carson.

Other WIAL colleagues must be recognized: Paulina Chu, Choon Seng Ng, Jayan Warrier, Shannon Banks, Joanne Irving, Martha Lappin, Jacqueline Villefane, Barbara Schaffer, and Jennifer Whitcomb who served with us on the WIAL Board of Directors as we developed a growing network of action learning team coaches that were trained in WIAL's approach to action learning team coaching.

Many people over the years have contributed to our knowledge and thinking about Action Learning as well as action-based (experiential) learning, executive coaching, team development, and organizational diagnosis and change: Barry Oshry, Bob Chin, David Glass, John Borriello, Ron Lippitt, Ken Benne, Erika Fromm, Phil Hanson, Chris Argyris, Dante Santora, Harry Levinson, Richard Kilburg, Bob Lee, Marc Sokol, Cori Hill, and David Peterson.

We also recognize Jim Champaign who provided enormous help in editing this manuscript. Finally, we are thankful to those around the globe who assisted in the production of this book - Kiran Naseer (Pakistan, book cover design), Julie Csizmadia (USA, interior layout and design), Nadia Pupa (USA, graphic development).

Foreword

Complex systems change refers to intentional modifications in how an organization, as a system, does business that affects strategic direction and competitive position (Smith, 2002). Smith points out that, as an organizational systems or subsystems leader, you are likely to be confronted by one or more of the following complex, transformational, discontinuous changes: mergers and acquisitions; expansion into new territory or lines of business; developing a customer-service organizational culture; a new system-wide software platform system like an ERP or CRM; process reengineering; new technology like robotics; total quality management (TQM); or a new business strategy.

It is not an easy decision for any leader to undertake the planning and implementation of significant and complex organizational changes. Leaders like you must first assess both the need for change and your organization's readiness for such change. Moreover, your decision must include: establishing meaningful and compelling change objectives; creating viable change strategies; and developing actionable implementation plans.

In addition, you must be willing to mobilize and deploy requisite talent and resources; monitor and assess on-going progress; and deal with unexpected consequences and predictable surprises during implementation. Finally, you need to evaluate and – whenever possible, necessary, and desirable – act on the results.

Once you make each of these decisions, you must make sure that involved parties or stakeholders are emotionally invested in and supportive of the decisions. Toward that end, it is vitally important for you to create meaningful opportunities for the full participation and involvement by all relevant parties -- wherever appropriate – in making and executing those decisions.

However, prerequisite to these decisions is another choice that is of the greatest magnitude. That is: Will you augment your own analyses and decisions by seeking assistance from people who have experience, knowledge, and behavioral skills in planning and implementing complex systems change? If so, you must choose which types and kinds of external consultants to hire – that is, unless you already have a full complement of fully qualified and experienced internal consultants. Many organizational leaders select consultants on the basis of referrals from trusted associates. This is a risky practice unless you have a very good idea about the types and kinds of consultants that are out there and what value you, as their employer and manager, can realistically expect each of them. Thus, Part I of this book provides you with a series of questionnaires and decision trees that will enable you to make realistic, wise decisions about consultants.

If you have already decided that you need and want action learning, Part I may not be directly relevant. So, you may choose to move directly to Part II. However, Part I may serve as a review that could confirm or challenge your choice of action learning. Or, Part I may demonstrate that you need a variety of consultants to fully support your complex systems change initiative. The larger and more complex your organizational systems change, the greater is the probability that you will require the services of different kinds and types of consultants. Once you have determined your needs, you can more easily determine where, how, and when to hire and deploy the different kinds of consultants.

In chapter 1, we discuss our descriptions of three types of problems and the core problem that is common to all change initiatives. In chapter 2, we consider the importance of making informed decisions regarding the selection of consultants. In chapter 3, we introduce the beginning of a decision tree and questionnaire to help you to determine if you need contract employees or extra-pairs-of-hands. In chapter 4, we add to the decision tree and provide another questionnaire to help you decide if your existing employees require education or training to enable them to manage your organizational change. In chapter 5, we add to the decision tree and offer another questionnaire to enable you to decide whether you need subject matter experts (SMEs) or technical expert (techspert) consultants to augment your organizational talent and their capacities. In chapter 6, we raise the extremely important question: Do you want to just solve the problem that confronts your organization right now or do you want to enable teams of your employees to create solutions and learn how to deal with future unprecedented and discontinuous problems? Another addition to the decision tree and a new questionnaire will help you clarify this choice. Finally, in chapter 7, using the last addition to the decision tree and the final questionnaire, we help you to compare the familiar task or process facilitator role with that of the action learning coach and guide you to making a choice between these two types of consultants.

We presume that when you finish Part I, you will be interested in learning more about leading, planning, and managing action learning projects. An action learning project would consist of four or more action learning teams working simultaneously on four or more different problems. If you have three or less action learning teams, the complexity of leading, planning, and managing them is considerably less. You may simply delegate one of your high potential senior managers to coordinate a small group of action learning teams. However, keep in mind that there will be the same complex challenges as presented in Part II, but at a smaller scale (Freedman & Stinson, 2004). Complexity is increased further if the action learning project is intended to augment or take the lead in a leadership development program or a complex organizational systems change initiative. So, in Part II, we provide you, the organizational leader, with a view of the context in which action learning projects are planned and implemented. In each chapter we define the tasks, activities, and functions that you must perform yourself or that you must ensure are performed in order to lead and support the initiative.

In chapter 8, we consider the nature of a proper "problem" that is best suited for action learning. The selected problem is the primary element of any radical, unprecedented, transformational change. In chapter 9, we describe the roles and the dynamics of the action learning team as it operates in the context of your organizational system and its component subsystems during a complex systems change. In chapter 10, we describe the primary operational principles of action learning: questioning and reflection. This is presented in some detail to make sure you understand and embrace the significance of these principles. This is essential since your continuing support of the application of these principles is critical to the success of an action learning project. In chapter 11, we present our conviction that you and other organizational leaders must express your active and visible support for the continuing commitment of all involved parties to taking action throughout the action learning process. In chapter 12, we discuss the need for support from all directly and indirectly involved parties in your organizational system for their sustained commitment to continuous learning in addition to creating proposed solutions. In chapter 13, we present an in-depth description of the tasks, activities, and functions of the action learning team coach. This will help all organizational leaders to understand, accept, and support the action learning coach's role and responsibilities. Finally, we present our summary and conclusions, including our invitation to call on us to provide reliable advice regarding your current or proposed organizational change initiatives.

A Cautionary Tale. A Google search will undoubtedly reveal extensive theories and models for organizational change. If you already have a working relationship with management consultants, you will have discovered that they are guided by their own theoretical model for change strategies and plans. They may say these mental models are proprietary; they may or may not be willing to share their mental models with you or your subordinate managers. This guardedness will create additional, unnecessary complications. Your people will be blind to their guiding principles and beliefs. So, you have no choice but to put yourselves in their hands and keep the *faith* that they know what they are doing to and for you and your organizational system. Keep in mind that these, like all mental models (including ours), are biased in some way. For example, many subject matter experts (SMEs) focus only on their core technologies and ignore or avoid the human element and systemic perspectives. In order to balance this bias, forward-looking executives should make themselves intimately familiar with at least two comprehensive models for planning and leading organizational change (see Freedman, 2013). Then you will have a choice. Otherwise, you can only accept the existing model or the status quo.

Accordingly, you should use an acceptable mental model of organizations to help you to understand and prepare to deal with the impacts that planning and implementing change are likely to have on your existing organizational system and its interdependent subsystems, as well as how your organization's culture might impact (and be impacted by) the complex systems change project.

In addition to the internal talent of an organization, complex systems change initiatives often require a variety of external resources to insure overall effectiveness. This might require the hiring of contract employees (extra-pairs-of-hands), trainer-educators, SMEs or technical experts (techsperts), as well as consulting organizational psychologists (COPs) or organization development and change (OD&C) practitioners. Such COPs or OD&C practitioners are usually proficient in task or process facilitation and should be (but are not all) proficient in action learning (team) coaching. Part I will help you to determine which kinds of consultants you may need at various phases of your project.

However, before you authorize a change project that leads with or includes action learning, you should understand and agree with the conditions that will insure your project's effectiveness. This is critical since it will be your responsibility to visibly, continuously support these conditions. Accordingly, we offer a great deal of useful information and guidance regarding how to improve and strengthen contemporary organizations primarily through the process of action learning.

The Use of "You." We use the pronoun, "you" in several contexts. First, "you" may be taken as singular or plural since "you" may be a CEO or a member of the C-suite. "You" may refer to an executive or middle management team. "You" may be the leader of a division, region, or product group. "You" may be a director of a staff department, senior manager in a major subsystem, manager, or supervisor. "You" may be the leader of an organizational change project management team. "You" may be a representative of one of the organization's major stakeholder groups. Or, "you" may be an unofficial opinion leader. In any event, you are in a powerful position to exert considerable influence in the various decisions that organizations make as they deal with the challenge of critical, radical, transformational, unprecedented, complex systems changes.

When we say, "You must or should or might" do some thing, we do not necessarily believe that you should personally make every specific decision or personally take every specific action that we recommend. We do, however, mean that it is you who will ultimately be responsible for the decisions or the actions and their consequences. You certainly may choose to delegate many of these decisions and actions to your direct reports or staff members. This puts your associates in visible positions in support of the complex systems change effort along with you. This can be a developmental experience for them. This may also increase their emotional investment and commitment to support your decisions and plans as a consequence of their active involvement and participation in their development and dissemination to the entire organization. We wrote this book is to provide you with as much information as we can to assure that you contribute to making intelligent, *informed decisions*.

PART I.
IDENTIFYING THE LEADER

Organizational systems exist in the public or private sector. They might also be non-profit or non-governmental organizations (NGOs). Leadership roles and positions are found at various levels: the executive director of the total organization or at the senior and middle manager levels of significant subsystems. In fact, people who lead any subsystem are leaders. You may lead a region, product group, division, department, or intact work unit. You may even be an informal opinion leader. Executive management teams (EMTs) are composed of senior line leaders of major subsystems and may include senior directors of staff functions like human resource management, financial services, or legal services. Board of directors may be composed of a mix of internal employees that may include labor and/or external retired or current executives of various organizations. EMTs and boards may have broad or specific leadership responsibilities and prerogatives.

The organization itself may be local, national, international, or global in scope. Leaders might be based at the organization's headquarters or in their satellite operations anywhere in the world. These leaders probably have both profit-and-loss responsibility and the discretionary authority to assess and improve the effectiveness of their system or subsystem within the organization.

In truth, no organization is an independent, autonomous entity. Leaders are very conscious of how existing systems affect and are affected by their interactions with a network of interdependent subsystems within their larger organization. Moreover, leaders are probably also aware that specific organizational systems are embedded in a constantly changing network of stakeholders that exist in the external environment with which they are tightly interdependent. It is apparent that the organization is affected by changes in these external stakeholders' conditions and activities and, in turn, may affect those stakeholders.

This becomes increasingly clear when external or internal environmental conditions change, in which case the larger organizational system and its component subsystems must also change so as to either eliminate or minimize emerging threats or to capitalize on fortuitous opportunities.

Leaders know that organizations consist of interdependent specialized subsystems, each of which is supposed to be best suited to deal with different kinds of routine work as well as with changes in the organization's internal and external environments. Boundary-spanning subsystems such as procurement, marketing, sales, human resource management, and strategic planning are among the subsystems most likely to provide early warnings of any changes that might be emerging or intensifying in the external environment. Leaders are aware that when one subsystem changes how it operates in order to adapt and cope with changing external conditions, it also changes its interactions with its related interdependent subsystems – and that forces these related subsystems to make secondary or tertiary adaptive changes.

Under such circumstances, leaders like you may be acutely aware that changing internal or external conditions create problems of different levels of urgency, complexity, importance, and familiarity in various parts and levels of the organization. Nonetheless, competent leaders usually feel confident that they (and other organizational members) have mastered a repertoire of problem solving methods and procedures that have been effective in dealing with familiar problems that are of low or moderate levels of urgency, complexity, and importance.

However, as the problems become more discontinuous with system leaders' past experiences and are more urgent, complex, and important, the organization's existing problem-solving procedures and capacities become less relevant and less effective. This becomes particularly evident when multiple impacts of a variety of challenging, unprecedented environmental changes occur simultaneously or in close proximity. This causes additional problems since, most often, organizations have limited resources available to fully address emerging problems while also maintaining the routine performance levels of a subsystem.

An Identifiable Help Line. We are consulting organizational psychologists (COPs) with long histories of performing a variety of consultative functions in service to myriad client organizations around the world. Accordingly, as shown in this book, *we are prepared to provide you with unparalleled consulting services. Our key strategy is to offer leaders like you with unique, relevant, trustworthy services* that will deliver maximum advantages at minimum costs and minimum confusion. We collaborate quite well with SMEs, many kinds of techsperts, and trainer-educators. And, recognizing that planned transformational change efforts fail to achieve their intended objectives from 60% to 70% of the time (Beer & Nohria, 2000; Grady, Magda, & Grady, 2011; IBM, 2008; Keller & Price, 2011; Kotter, 1998; Senge, 1999; Standish Group, 2009; and Strebel, 1998), we want you to understand the kinds of services that will *increase the probability that your projects will be successful.*

As such, in Part I, we help you to make informed decisions about the fit between your organization's needs and available consulting services. We want you to choose us for assistance in learning how to solve critical complex systems change problems while enhancing your own and your employees' leadership behavior, participative teamwork, and organizational systems change skills. We expect that in the process, you will increase your value to the organization considerably by leading it through action learning, real-time leadership growth and development, and meaningful organizational changes.

In Part II, we provide considerable information about the complex dynamics and leadership responsibilities involved in leading, planning, and managing complex systems change using action learning.

This approach to solving problems while simultaneously developing leadership skills and enabling organizational change gives credible nuance to the phrase that Freedman coined some years ago:

Experience is the test that is followed by the lesson.

CHAPTER 1.

Identifying the Critical Problems

Whenever an organization's future is challenged by a number of serious problems, it is incumbent on leadership to determine the causes. Radical changes in elements of an organization's external environment might be responsible for an outcropping of serious problems that demand adaptive internal organizational shifts. For example, major changes in local or national economic conditions, new technology, competition, acquisitions, manmade or natural disasters, governmental regulations, or changing customer or employee demographics and preferences can have an adverse impact on the success of a long-standing organization.

On the other hand, some problems can be traced to internal causes such as the breakdown of a major mechanical or technological element, low morale, or underperformance.

No matter the cause, such problems are critical and complex; viable solutions are urgently needed. Moreover, it is likely that these problems are unprecedented. Whether the problems are rooted in or result from external or internal shifts and changes matters little. Indeed, the fact of their novelty, as well as their volume and types might call for radical and dramatic responses (Freedman, 1997). This is true particularly because leaders probably became aware of the problems and their implications only gradually.

The problems –although new – might originate from any of three underlying conditions. First, some system, structure, or process breaks down or seems to be seriously underperforming; this needs to be *fixed*. Second, an unexpected, unprecedented opportunity emerges that could benefit you, one or several of your subsystems, or your organization as a whole. Opportunities need to be *exploited* or capitalized upon.

There is yet a third category to consider: Some problems that you might believe were dealt with previously can reemerge and have to be dealt with over and over. No enduring solution has been found. Rather, the same problem recurs in the same or a similar form. This may be called a dilemma (Johnson, 1992) For example, systemic inefficiencies may have been revealed that led to a decision to decentralize some line and staff functions. That may have worked effectively – for a while. However, over time, decentralization produced a number of new, unacceptable side effects. So, leaders might decide to re-centralize some functions and leave others decentralized. That can work for a while, but more unexpected consequences might emerge. So the process repeats itself. Such recurring dilemmas may not ever be solved permanently. These dilemmas might have to be *managed* by making continuing adjustments.

You may have gradually come to the realization that *the core problem* is not so much the existence of any one or combination of these three underlying conditions. It is more likely that your organization's core problem is that it cannot function at an optimally effective level until you and your associates figure out *how* to move from the unacceptable underlying current-state condition to some collectively agreeable, compelling goal or desired state.

You might have applied your organization's existing problem-solving managerial procedures and processes to the problem. Unfortunately, such applications probably produced results that at best were only temporary, ineffective, superficial, or put band-aids on obvious symptoms rather than solve the underlying root causes. The critical problem may be exacerbated because you, the management team, and/or the organizational system itself lack the requisite information, knowledge, or proficiency in applying methods, procedures, and skills to deal effectively with critically important, unprecedented, discontinuous problems.

Furthermore, you might have tried to augment your own resources by directing subordinates – or staff subsystems like human resource management – to search for and apply *best practices* that have been developed by other organizations to deal with similar problems in different contexts. However, these best practices often do not fit well or are rejected by organizational members – remember the "not invented here" phenomenon. This can give rise to increased tension and frustration and subsequent feelings of disappointment with leaders for not figuring out how to deal with the unprecedented problems.

You might also feel distressed by an increasing number and variety of recriminations as colleagues deflect criticism away from themselves.

As dissatisfaction with current conditions increases, energy builds up and pushes you and your associates to search for and discover new perspectives and creative new alternatives for moving the organization effectively, from *here* – the current state – to *there* – the desired state. That is true problem solving that can become a major organizational strength. That is where action learning may be essential.

By its nature, action learning is a first step toward enabling you and your organizational members to learn how to create enduring solutions.

CHAPTER 2.

Informed Action Learning Decisions

Needs and Preferences. To make informed decisions, you need relevant, timely, and reliable information about what you need to deal effectively with the focal issues confronting you. Unfortunately, too many leaders convince themselves that they and their executive management team members, alone, have all the pertinent information they need to make high quality decisions. This is an illusion.

While a team of managers may make higher quality collective decisions than those made by any given individual manager, teams need to take it to the next level. Teams must first surface and then verify or disconfirm the assumptions its members make as they strive to come to a consensus. To assess the validity of management teams' decision, they must collect additional information from a broad range of the teams' *stakeholders.* Indeed, the larger the number and types of different perspectives help to insure greater comprehensiveness and accuracy of their decision-making.

However, *what is needed* is often quite different from what management teams *prefer*. Preferences are strongly influenced by individual and collective past experiences. You and your colleagues may find comfort and too much confidence in whatever is familiar. Accordingly, you may be suspicious of anything that is strange – even when that may be exactly what it will take to resolve important problems.

This book seeks to convert what might be ambiguous, unknown and suspicious to something that is comprehensible, credible, and effective. The key is to make fully informed decisions about the variety and numbers of consultants you will need to recruit, select, and deploy to help you to implement your complex systems change. This will involve making use of the informative questionnaires and decision-trees that are presented in the next few chapters.

We recommend using the questionnaires and decision trees in the following manner:

First, you and your closest associates should individually rate the options in each questionnaire, one by one. Then, sit down with your associates and share your responses. Note the similarities in ratings. Pay close attention to those comparisons where there are significant differences in your ratings. Discuss these differences with your associates. What led some people to rate an item one way while others rated the same item quite differently? What personal experiences, theories, or beliefs led individuals to rate items as they did? During these discussions, your task is to listen, ask questions, and understand people who disagree with you as *they* want to be understood. Refrain from arguing or trying to influence people to agree with you. More often than not, you will discover that, with open and honest dialog, people who disagree with one another can still understand and appreciate other people's logic and points of view – even if they do not agree with one another. With mutual respect, people with divergent opinions and beliefs can come to mutually agreeable, near-consensus choices. In some cases, you may want to reach out to some of your subordinates and stakeholders to include their opinions.

Once you have a reasonably broad base of agreement for each of the following questionnaires, you will quite easily be able to make very well informed decisions about the proper types of consultants you will need.

CHAPTER 3.

The Limits of Workers and Time

Leaders like you often explain shortcomings of any subsystem's response to sudden, critical changes with your perceived need for more workers and/or more time. The notion that a coherent business unit is *stretched too thin and/or needs more time and/or more people to handle a specific challenge* is a common response to problems that arise during both routine operations and exceptional circumstances.

The first step in confronting that type of situation requires extensive self-examination – without recrimination, anger or guilt. This can be accomplished best by establishing some base-line data through the use of questionnaires [See Table 3.1 below]. Remember, you and your direct reports should first answer this questionnaire individually, then compare results, discuss areas of disagreement, and create a single set of responses.

Requesting additional, temporary help is probably the safest way to improve the viability of any group or organization when change consists of an increase in the *volume* of well-known tasks, activities, or functions that overloads the existing workforce *and* when there is a pool of qualified but unemployed *and* accessible workers who are willing to work on a temporary basis. Extra-pairs-of-hands are also appropriate options if leaders need to increase the *speed* of processing the normal flow of work on a full time but temporary basis.

Table 3.1. Do you need an extra-pair-of-hands?
Instructions: Think about the situation in your organization for which you are considering enlisting some help from external or internal consultants. Use the five-point scale below to rate how well each of the six statements describes the situation. **5** = An excellent description of our current situation **4** = A good description **3** = A fairly accurate description **2** = A poor description **1** = This does not describe our current situation in any respect

Statement	5	4	3	2	1
1. Your existing employees cannot deal with the temporarily high volume or variety of work.	5	4	3	2	1
2. The consultants are intended to be a strictly temporary addition to the existing workforce due to a short-term, non-recurring demand for their knowledge, skills, and aptitudes.	5	4	3	2	1
3. The consultants are expected to fit into the existing workforce and function as full- or part-time – but temporary – producers.	5	4	3	2	1
4. Permanent line managers determine exactly what the consultants are expected to do and, to a large extent, how they are to do it.	5	4	3	2	1
5. Consultants are expected to accept the objectives and schedules given by the organization's permanent managers.	5	4	3	2	1
6. Line managers actively supervise the consultants as they perform the tasks, activities, or functions for which they were engaged.	5	4	3	2	1

7. The consultant's performance will be evaluated against the same standards that are used to evaluate the performance of permanent employees occupying the same positions.	5	4	3	2	1
TOTAL SCORE					

Total the points that you have given to each of the seven statements above and record your total in the space provided.

Total points: If your points total 28 or more, this clearly indicates that you are seeking an extra-pair-of-hands consultant. A total of 14 or less clearly indicates that the organization may be better served by one of the other three consultant types. Scores between 15 and 27 are mid-range scores that indicate that some extra-pairs-of-hands are needed, but, by themselves, will be insufficient to solve the problem.

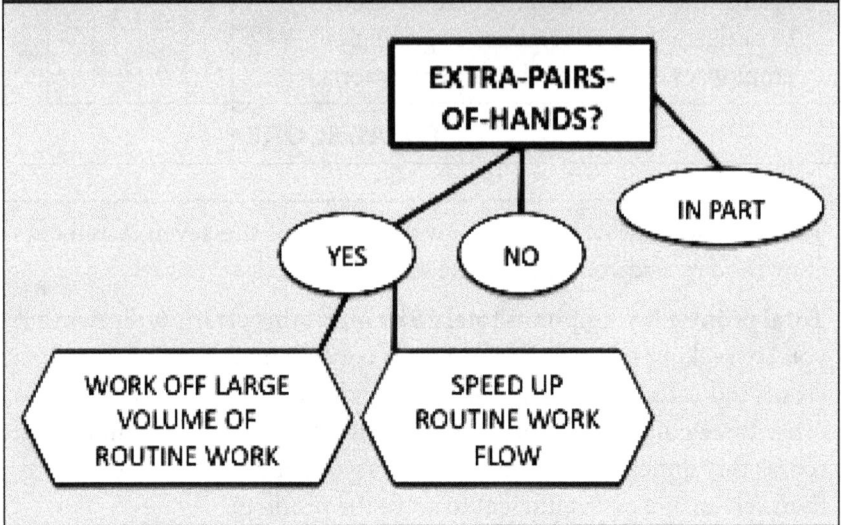

Figure 3.1. Do You Need Extra-Pairs-of-Hands?

As indicated in Figure 3.1, it might be that you could use *some* extra-pairs-of-hands, particularly to relieve some permanent employees from their routine responsibilities so you can redeploy them to help deal with challenging unprecedented changes. So, hiring extra-pairs-of-hands might prove to be a necessary, albeit insufficient and partial strategy that would *supplement* some other kind of intervention more likely to solve the problem.

The Real Dilemma When you determine that the assistance needed goes beyond just merely adding to the existing workforce temporarily, a critical challenge ensues. To wit: You might think that asking for help might be seen by your colleagues or stakeholders as an admission of your incompetence. In deference to this possibility, you might decide to wait until the need for dealing with the change subsides. But this strategy entails major risks. For one thing, waiting for a fixed number of employees to work off a large volume of work causes delays. Delays often create frustration and disappointment among customers who are then likely to turn to your competitors for faster service. For another thing, the need to deal with the change may not diminish or go away.

You might choose instead to take a more proactive approach and consult with your peers in other organizations to see how they manage turbulent conditions within and across their own subsystems. If you learn that you are not the only executive experiencing problems, it is likely that you, despite some indications of increased tension and, perhaps, anxiety, might think it would be unwise to be the first to say anything as this could entail the risk of "losing face." Still, informed and forward-looking leaders will usually understand that things won't get better by themselves. In that situation, they are apt to willingly take the risk of acknowledging that a new type of systemic challenge exists. We often ask our executive clients who are dealing with this dilemma:

"Are you so weak that you have to look strong?
Or, are you strong enough to appear to look weak?"

CHAPTER 4.

The Need for Competency Training

Once you recognize the need to fix something that is broken or is underperforming, the next logical and compelling step is for you to take the courageous risk of asking for help. Assuming you have the necessary discretionary authority and as well as the budget to accomplish the task at hand, you must address the question of *what kind of consultative assistance will best resolve the problem*

In discussions with peers and superiors, you might find that in all too many cases, they implicitly assume that the reason performance is suffering is that some employees simply do not know what to do and/or how to do it. If this assumption is valid, it suggests that what you need is a knowledgeable, experienced subject matter expert (SME) who is also a skilled *trainer-educator* who can enable workers to master the knowledge, skills, and aptitudes necessary to cope with changing conditions. Further, the implicit assumption may be that, once they have mastered the requisite competencies, employees will be less anxious and more motivated to do their jobs as expected. As indicated in Figure 4.1, below, you might determine that extra-pairs-of-hands are only part of the total solution. Additional training and education of existing workers and their managers might enable them to create their own viable solution to the problem.

But, you will have to decide what kind of training your employees should get. Training programs that teach systematic problem solving methods, like the Kepner-Tregoe system (1997) may be too rigid to apply to multiple incidences of rapidly changing conditions. Programs that help people to develop high performing, innovative teams need to be considered (see, for example, Hackman, 2002, 2011).

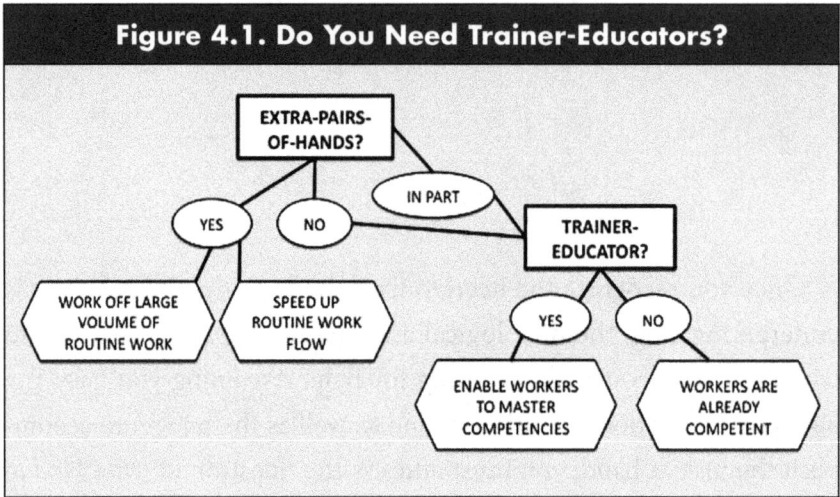

Figure 4.1. Do You Need Trainer-Educators?

Your decision to invest in this kind of intervention should rest on an evaluation of answers to the questions contained in Table 4.1 *"Do You Need a Training/Educational Specialist?"* (below). Remember, you and your associates and direct reports should first answer this questionnaire individually, then compare results, discuss areas of disagreement, and create a single set of responses.

The first question is particularly important. How can you know with any degree of certainty whether or not workers already possess the essential information, conceptual knowledge, and behavioral/technical skills needed to effectively respond to organizational changes. Some employees might be fully or partly competent but have not been encouraged or rewarded for using their knowledge and skills. In fact, some competent employees might have been subjected to social pressure or otherwise prevented from using their knowledge, and skills.

However, since you may not have witnessed the type of competencies that are both needed and expected, it is too easy to assume your employees do not have it. Before leaping to that conclusion, you must understand that to invest scarce resources in training people who are already competent can be a disaster. Therefore, you are obliged to look deeper to determine if employees do or do not have the requisite competencies. One way of looking deeper requires using a focused questionnaire that underscores the question: *"Could they do it if their lives depended on it?"* (Mager & Pipe, 1997). Another way is reflected in question 3 that suggests a controlled study of a representative sample of employees.

Table 4.1. The Need for Training-Educational Specialists

Instructions: This questionnaire contains eleven questions. Use the five-point scale below to rate how well each statement describes the specific situation for which you are considering hiring a consultant.

5 = An excellent description of our current situation
4 = A good description
3 = A fairly accurate description
2 = A poor description
1 = This does not describe our current situation in any respect

1. Employees do not display competent use of essential information, conceptual knowledge or theory, and/or behavioral or technical skills.	5	4	3	2	1
2. Information, knowledge or theory, and/or skills that our employees do not seem to possess are needed on a continual basis, both now and in the future.	5	4	3	2	1
3. A representative sample of the employees in question have voluntarily taken part in a controlled experiment to determine if they actually have mastered the needed knowledge and skills. Less than 15% show proficiency in the needed competencies.	5	4	3	2	1
4. Employees who are to be trained are highly motivated and are eager to be provided with an opportunity to learn.	5	4	3	2	1
5. The managers of the individuals to be trained make sure they have little difficulty in applying and making use of their new information, knowledge or theory, and/or skills in performing their role responsibilities.	5	4	3	2	1

6. Executive management takes concrete, visible steps to support, reinforce, and reward individuals as they apply the knowledge and skills gained from the training.	5	4	3	2	1
7. Executive management identifies and removes or minimizes any obstacles that might interfere with employees as they apply the new information, knowledge or theory, and/or skills in their work setting.	5	4	3	2	1
8. Training or educational activities have minimal disruptive effects on the tasks, activities, functions, or processes that are essential for the organization's current operations.	5	4	3	2	1
9. Organizational leaders believe that training and educational activities are worth temporary disruptions to routine operations that might occur.	5	4	3	2	1
10. Executive management believes the value derived from training and educating employees is greater than the costs.	5	4	3	2	1
11. Executive management believes there is a good probability that, over time, the costs of training or education will be recouped in the form of tangible increases in organizational effectiveness.	5	4	3	2	1
TOTAL SCORE					

Add the points that you have given to each of the eleven statements and write the total in the space indicated.

Total points: A total of 44 or above is a clear indication that you believe that training or education will benefit employees. Scores of 22 or less are a good indication that training-education is not needed.

It is possible that training or educational specialists might be useful if your total is from 23 to 43 points, especially if they are capable of helping participants and their managers to clarify and deal with the post-training issues (indicated by statements 3 through 10). Within this range, you should supplement your training or educational specialists with COPs or OD&C practitioners.

There is one critical caveat in using this questionnaire. That is: How can you know for sure that your answers to questions 1 and 2 are valid? After all, if employees are not rewarded or if they are punished if they do attempt to apply their knowledge, skills, and aptitudes, you, their supervisors, and their colleagues are unlikely to know that they have competencies that they are not using. Therefore, keep in mind the idea that just because you don't see the competencies does not mean they are not there. They may be hidden. If this is the case, you have an organizational cultural problem, not a competency problem. That is, the cultural values of your organization do not accept the introduction of new information, knowledge, or skills into the workplace. Anyone who violates this norm elicits social pressure, coercion, or intimidation aimed at discouraging such actions. This suggests a cultural change intervention, not training or education.

This does not mean that training or education is totally irrelevant. At least some of your employees and managers may benefit from some targeted technical education and behavioral skills training in addition to extra-pairs-of-hands, and other types of consultants. Your job is to make sure that people get what they need, not what they do not need.

CHAPTER 5.

Depending on Experts or Increasing Your Organization's Capacities

Some of your peers might suggest that you look in a different direction than training and education. You might determine that both workers and managers are already technically and managerially competent and, therefore, do not require training or education.

As indicated in Figure 5.1 below, your peers might suggest that a SME or techspert consultant is needed to explain, diagnose, either correct or prevent a problem, or recommend a solution for a problem that you or your employees are to execute. In this case the background and competencies of the techspert consultant should match the nature of the problems in the workplace. The consultant also should have experience either in applying their own well-known solutions or be capable of creating effective new solutions. Creating effective solutions is far more complex and demanding than simply picking an off-the-shelf solution.

Under the circumstances, what is unfamiliar, uncertain, and ambiguous to you and your colleagues or immediate subordinates should be clear and familiar to the techspert consultant. Your peers might argue further that the consultant should have special experience with your industry and the specific functions of its subsystems. While this might sound reasonable, this last point might not be a valid assumption. Still, by finding someone who satisfies these criteria, you can reasonably expect to avoid making most embarrassing and costly mistakes.

The techspert should, in many ways, *absorb your ambiguity*. Accordingly, you can expect that the techspert consultant will fix – or explain to you and your employees how to fix – what is broken, push performance rates higher, determine how to exploit opportunities, and/or demonstrate how to manage recurring dilemmas.

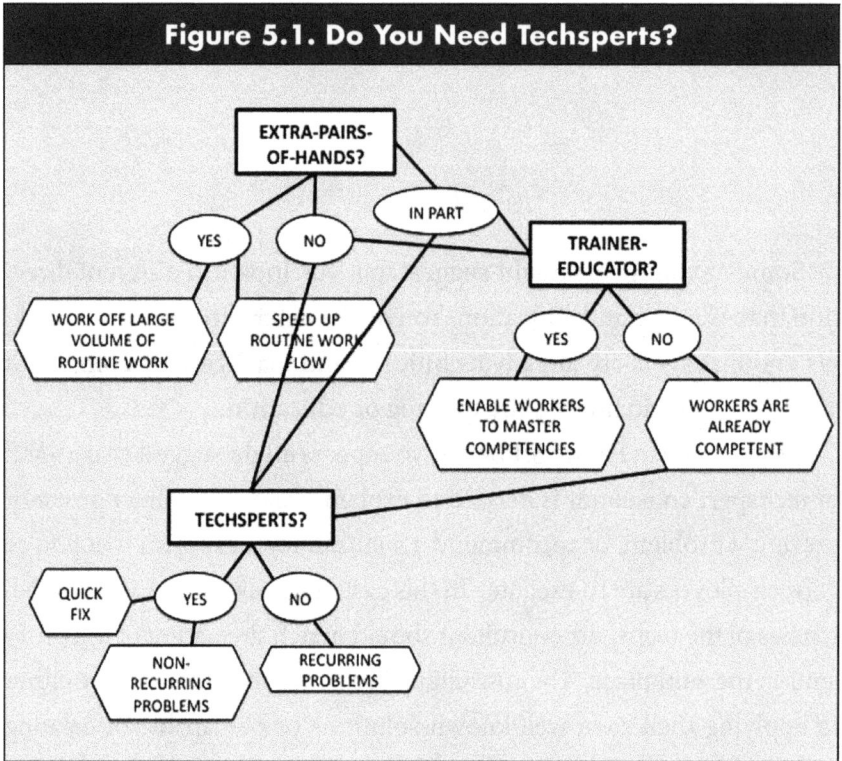

Figure 5.1. Do You Need Techsperts?

You should be concerned about what, if anything, a selected tech-spert or SME consultant might leave behind after helping to solve the problem. Your concern should hinge on the question of whether or not the problem is likely to recur in the future. If the answer is yes, you might consider further whether you need to develop and expand your employees' existing capacity to solve such problems by themselves, without costly external consultative assistance. However, if you believe that this kind of problem will not recur, you would prudently conclude that you could always call the techspert back in if the problem recurs. In this case there is no reason to train employees to master the necessary competencies.

However, as indicated in Figure 5.1, if this or similar problems are likely to recur, techsperts would not be the most prudent choice. Neither would extra-pairs-of-hands or trainer-educators. You need consultants who can help employees to not only solve the current problem but also help them to acquire and master the competencies they will need in the future. For this, you will need either a COP or an OD&C practitioner. Such consultants are not techsperts. They are, however, experts in helping organizational members solve real problems in real time while, secondarily, helping them to develop and apply powerful problem-solving competencies. When needed for their substantive contributions, techsperts and SMEs can generally be brought in on a temporary basis to work with COPs and OD&C practitioners.

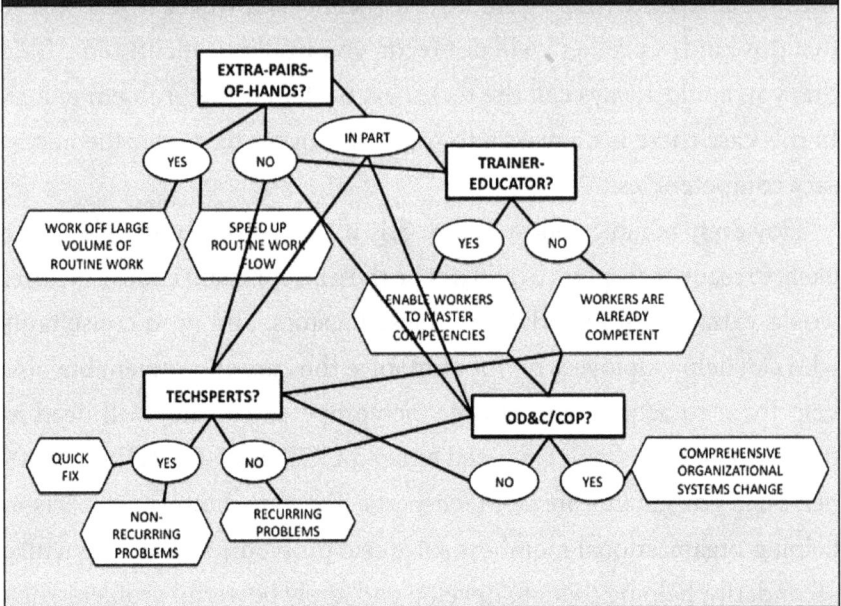

Figure 5.2. Do You Need OD&C Practitioners or COP consultants?

Furthermore, regarding which type of consultant – techsperts, COPs or OD&C consultants – will best serve your and your management team's needs and preferences, you might find it useful to answer the questions in Table 5.1 (below). Remember, once again, you and your direct reports should first answer this questionnaire individually, then compare results, discuss areas of disagreement, and create a single set of responses.

Table 5.1. Do you need techsperts or consulting organizational psychologists (COPs) or OD&C practitioners?

Instructions: The following questionnaire contains 12 sections, each of which has two possible responses. Your task is to choose which of the two options is closest to your understanding of the situation.

When evaluating each pair of responses, think about the specific project for which you are considering hiring a consultant. What do you want, need, and expect the consultant to do for your organization? Think about what is best for your organization in the short term *and* in the long run. What kind of a working relationship do you want or need between you, the members of your organization, and your consultants?

1. The nature of the issue:

A. The problem confronting your organization is one-of-a-kind and is not likely to recur. There is no advantage in acquiring the competencies necessary to deal with similar problems in the future. You expect consultants to recommend a solution or to solve the problem and achieve the results you need.

B. Similar issues are likely to occur in the future. Therefore, you expect consultants to collaborate with organization managers and other members in dealing with the issue while simultaneously enhancing your employees' competence to deal with similar issues in the future.

2. Determination of goals and methods:

A. Your organization's managers determine the *goals* to be achieved by your consultants; the consultants will determine the best *methods* for reaching these goals.

B. Management *and* consultants jointly determine what goals are to be achieved through the consulting effort and what strategies, actions, and methods are to be used to achieve these goals.

3. Consultant/client relationship:
A. Developing a relationship between managers and consultants is not a significant factor. You need to trust consultants to provide viable solutions to the problem through the application of their specialized knowledge, skills, and procedures.
B. A high-trust, open relationship between managers and the consultants is essential. All parties must collaborate and exchange information in a transparent and timely manner throughout the consulting assignment to both solve the problem and develop your employees.

4. Reporting:
A. Consultants assume primary responsibility for the successful completion of all stages of the consulting assignment. But they may call on organizational members from time to time to assist, collect relevant information, or report progress.
B. Management and consultants share *joint* responsibility for the successful completion of the consulting assignment and must maintain continual contact.

5. Control:
A. Consultants have technical control over the project because they have more practical knowledge and experience than organizational members in this area. However, managers retain control over available resources, budgets, schedules, and logistics.
B. Managers share control with consultants by discussing and negotiating all issues that emerge.

6. Situation analysis:
A. Managers expect consultants to take full responsibility for analyzing the situation. Consultants decide what information is required, the methods to gather it, from whom, and how it will be organized, analyzed, and used.
B. Managers and consultants make joint decisions about what data will be collected, from whom, and how it will be organized, analyzed, and used.

7. Conclusions and recommendations:
A. Consultants derive conclusions from their analyses of the problems and use these as the basis for formulating concrete recommendations for correcting or improving the situation.
B. Managers, key organizational members, and consultants work together to draw conclusions from the collected and organized data, to specify and prioritize the issues, develop strategies, and formulate recommended action plans to deal with the selected issues.

8. Implementation of solution or action plans:
A. Consultants may either (a) provide management with their recommendations for solving the problem and/or (b) execute the technical solutions recommended.
B. Although managers take primary responsibility for execution, consultants may be actively involved as (a) coaches or shadow consultants or (b) members of a project management team. Consultants' roles are negotiated by managers and consultants as they jointly develop implementation plans.

9. Managing disagreements:
A. As experts in their field, consultants view any disagreements with organizational members as unjustified interference or lack of trust in their competence or professionalism.
B. Disagreements between organizational members and consultants are expected because of differences in goals, roles, responsibilities, backgrounds, and interests. Managers and consultants view differences as opportunities to learn from each other and also as sources of potential innovation.

10. Acceptance of consultant's recommendations:
A. Consultants expect their recommendations will be accepted quickly and implemented willingly by organizational members.
B. Consultants expect managers to provide assistance in gaining organizational members' acceptance, support, and commitment – particularly members who will be involved in the implementation process and those who will be affected by the implementation.

11. Evaluation of results:
A. Evaluation takes place at the conclusion of the consultation to determine whether consultants delivered what they promised. Consultants may write periodic progress reports for management.
B. Evaluations are conducted throughout the consultation to determine if adjustments to goals, strategies, and plans are needed. At a minimum, evaluations cover (a) progress being made, (b) the quality of results being achieved, (c) emerging issues – e.g., unexpected consequences and predictable surprises, (d) how emerging issues are handled, (e) the effectiveness of the efforts to handle the emerging issues, and (f) the effectiveness of the plan and implementation strategies and methods.

Evaluators:
A. Managers or someone designated by managers evaluates the quality, relevance, and effectiveness of consultant deliverables. Or, consultants are directed to evaluate their own work.
B. Managers hire objective third parties who have no other involvement with either the client organization or the consultants to conduct evaluations. Or, managers and consultants cooperate with third parties, jointly evaluating the emerging progress and results of the consultation.

Scoring

Circle your choices of each of the 12 alternatives above to the appropriate columns below. Then total your points in each column.

Although it is unlikely that the total points in either column will be zero, you will probably give more points to one or the other of the two consulting types. The results should illuminate which of the two types feels more appropriate to you. However, what *feels* more appropriate may not *be* the most appropriate.

	Techsperts	COPs/OD&C
1	A.	B.
2	A.	B.
3	A.	B.
4	A.	B.
5	A.	B.
6	A.	B.
7	A.	B.
8	A.	B.
9	A.	B.
10	A.	B.
11	A.	B.
12	A.	B.
TOTALS		

Interpretation

If you have 10 or more total points for either techsperts or COPs/OD&C practitioners, those are the type of consultants you believe you need most. The closer the number of total points in the two columns, the more likely it is that you believe you will need both kinds of consultants. For example, you may discover that your organization needs COPs or OD&C practitioners to cooperate with techspert consultants or training/educational specialists. In such instances, it would be appropriate to create a multidisciplinary consulting team composed of various kinds of techsperts, trainer-educators, and COPs and OD&C practitioners.

If the results of the answers to the questionnaire point to a clear need (or preference) for a techspert consultant, you will probably seek someone who is both an SME-techspert who is also capable of controlling and driving the effort to solve problems created by external or internal systemic changes.

Alternatively, the results of the questionnaire might reveal your felt need for a COP or OD&C practitioner. Under such circumstances, you will want to hire someone who follows or collaboratively crafts a plausible and teachable organizational change model to provide guidance for the project management team and workers through a didactic process that results in jointly developing and implementing strategies and plans to solve the problems created by change.

CHAPTER 6

Solving the Problem vs. Solving the Problem and Learning

At this point, you might be thinking that you have made all the correct decisions needed to determine what or who to search for to find the proper type (or mix of types) of consultants. Perhaps.

You can be even more precise. For instance, merely decided that COPs or OD&C practitioners are needed is not sufficient. This decision needs to be explored further. There are several variables to consider. First, are the problems to be solved familiar to the consultants? Do the consultants have histories of success in guiding clients through flexible yet reliable processes that lead to the creation of viable solutions? In addition to solving the problem, are the consultants prepared to work themselves out of a job (Freedman, 2009) by developing the competencies of organizational and subsystem members and, thereby, reduce their dependence on the consultant?

It is reasonable for you to expect that both COPs and OD&C practitioners are skilled task or process facilitators. The facilitator skill sets are fundamental for most competent organizational change agents.

However, not all COPs or OD&C practitioners are trained and certified as *action learning coaches*.

It is important for you to determine whether task or process facilitators or action learning coaches will best meet the needs of the organization. Or, perhaps, you will discover you need both sets of competencies. Toward that end, you should compare the methods used and probable results achieved by both types of consultants so as to deploy them appropriately. Consider the choices using the side-by-side comparisons in Table 6.1, below. Remember, once again, you and your direct reports should first answer this questionnaire individually, then compare results, discuss areas of disagreement, and create a single set of responses. Review the results to determine what type of consultant you really need.

On the surface, task/process facilitators and action learning (team) coaches appear to be quite similar in terms of what they contribute to the effectiveness of the teams to which they consult. The differences between the two types can, however, be discerned by the methods each employs and the results they help teams achieve.

Table 6.1. Need for task (or process) facilitators vs. action learning (team) coaches?

Instructions: The following questionnaire contains 11 sections, each of which has two possible responses. The task is to choose between the two alternatives within each section. Circle the letter ("A" or "B") to indicate which of the two options you believe is the most important.

When evaluating each pair of responses, reflect on the specific assignment for which you are considering hiring a consultant. What is it that you want, need, and expect the consultant to do for the organization? What do you want the consultants to deliver? Think about what is best for the organization in the short term and in the long run. What kind of a working relationship do you want or need between the members of the organization and the consultants?

1. Solutions:
A. Consultants actively participate in discussions with organizational members about the content of the problem; advocates particular goals, strategies, or solutions.
B. Consultants remain neutral; refrain from discussing the contents of the problem; do not advocate any goals, strategies, or solutions; consultants help organizational members set their own goals and create their own strategies and solutions.

2. Problem solving methods:
A. Consultants provide team with methods to solve problems when members are uncertain or confused about how to proceed thereby making sure team members avoid wasting time or make mistakes.
B. Consultants rely on team members to recall and apply their own known problem solving methods or to create new methods thereby learning to identify and use their own resources.

3. Focus:
A. Consultants focus on making sure the team solves the problem or completes the task.
B. Consultants help team members to focus on how well they are making progress, achieving results, and learning from the process.

4. Use of questions:
A. Consultants ask leading, yes/no, and/or multiple-choice questions based on their theories and opinions to direct team members to what the consultants believe are the proper responses and actions.
B. Consultants ask open-ended questions during divergent phases of team problem solving to elicit useful information; then use closed-ended questions during convergent phases to help the team agree on its options.

5. Statements:
A. Consultants make statements about content of the problem and team process to inform and guide the team.
B. Consultants may choose to respond to questions – but do not respond to questions about the problem's contents or the team's strategies, or action plans.

6. Conflict:
A. Consultants try to resolve, avoid, or suppress conflicts within the team or between the team and external stakeholders to help members move quickly beyond their differences.
B. Consultants help team to clarify emerging differences and to manage and use conflicts to enhance members' understanding and use of divergent opinions and interests of both team members and stakeholders.

7. Assumptions:
A. Consultants often accept or do not recognize or challenge assumptions thus saving team time.
B. Consultants inquire to help members or stakeholders make their assumptions explicit and to invite them to test the validity of their beliefs.

8. Resistance:
A. Consultants attempt to avoid or quickly overcome resistance.
B. Consultants inquire when resistance occurs to help team learn how to understand and use resistance to uncover useful information and move toward agreement.

9. Scope of attention:
A. Consultants focus on the presenting problem and its primary location.
B. Consultants focus on the primary as well as interdependent secondary and tertiary locations that may contribute to the problem and may be affected by the implementation and results of the solution.

10. Team problems:
A. Consultants move team along quickly by rescuing members when they get into difficulties.
B. Consultants let team struggle when it gets into difficulties so they discover that they can help themselves.

11. Dependency/self-reliance:	
	A. Consultants induce dependency of teams on them by taking responsibility for providing assistance and direction.
	B. Consultants encourage self-determination of teams by encouraging members to take risks, explore, discover, use its members' resources, innovate, and learn when they encounter unprecedented challenges.

Further Instructions: Circle either "A" or "B" for each of the 11 statements. Add the number of times you circled either "A" and "B" and write this number in the total columns.

	Facilitators	Coaches
1	A	B
2	A	B
3	A	B
4	A	B
5	A	B
6	A	B
7	A	B
8	A	B
9	A	B
10	A	B
11	A	B
TOTAL		

Interpretation:

If you have circled either "A" or "B" nine or more times, you are indicating a clear preference, one way or the other. That is, if you circles "A" nine or more times, you are expressing a firm opinion that you want a task or process facilitator as your consultant. This implies your belief that the task or process facilitator is the best type of consultant to enable your teams to realize their purpose.

On the other hand, if you indicated a clear preference for "B" nine or more times, you are expressing a firm belief that an action learning (team) coach will be the best type of consultant to help your teams to realize their purpose.

However, if you indicated that your preferences are more or less balanced between "A" and "B" – e.g., eight or less for "A" and three or more for "B," – it will be difficult for you to make a choice. You would seem to want some, but not all, of the functions performed by both styles. Consultants cannot perform the functions of both styles at the same time with the same team. Therefore, you are implying that you believe you need both types of consultants for different assignments.

If you recognize that there is a need for a task or process facilitator, you should be aware that almost all qualified and experienced COP and OD&C consultants are normally trained and are competent in providing this function.

Figure 6.1. Do You Need Task or Process Facilitators?

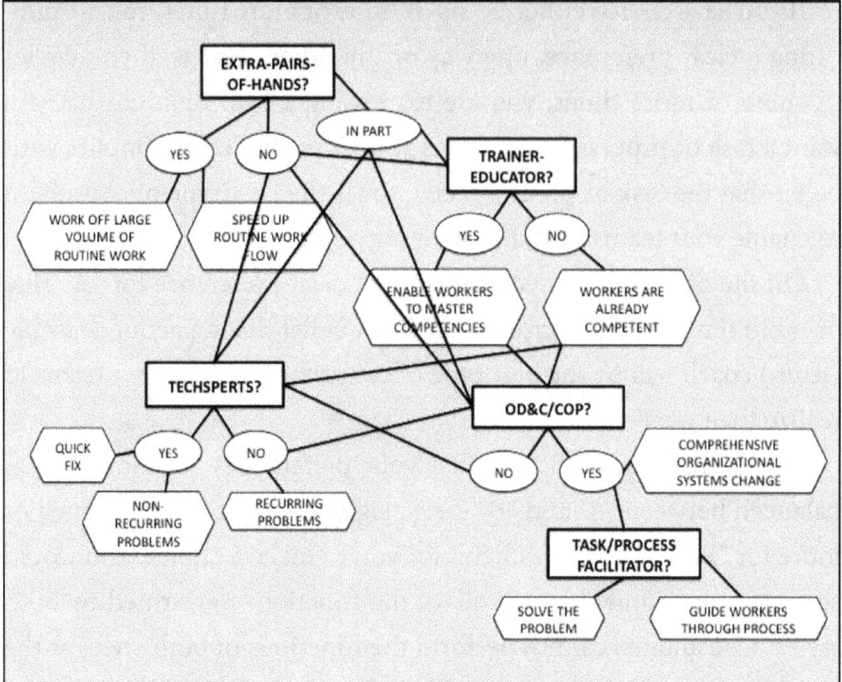

However, if the results of your responses to the questionnaire indicate that you really need action learning (team) coaches, you might encounter difficulties in searching for and selecting one that is fully qualified and certified. This is because many consultants claim they are competent action learning coaches but there is, to date, only one institute that trains and certifies action learning coaches: That is, the *World Institute for Action Learning* (www.WIAL.org).

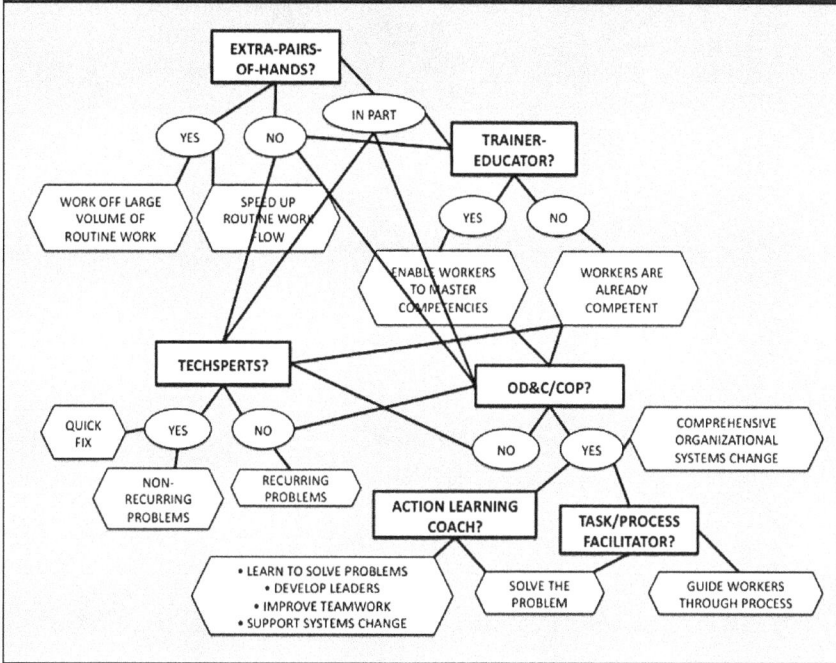

Figure 6.2. Do You Need Action Learning Coaches?

A Brief Summary. You can determine quickly which type of consultant you need by considering two factors:

First. What is known about the *project goals*?

Second. What is known about the *pathway (action plan) to the solution*?

As indicated in Figure 6.3, if the goals and the pathway are both clear and specific, what you probably need is a techspert or SME. If the project goal is ambiguous and unclear while the pathway is clear and specific, a task or process facilitator would be the better choice. For example, a task facilitator can guide an executive management team through well-established and reliable processes to enable them to create a viable strategic plan or gainsharing plan even though the outcomes are not clear to either the participants or the consultant at the beginning. The participants will create clarity and specificity for themselves as they are guided through such processes by the facilitator.

Figure 6.3. When to Use or Not Use Action Learning

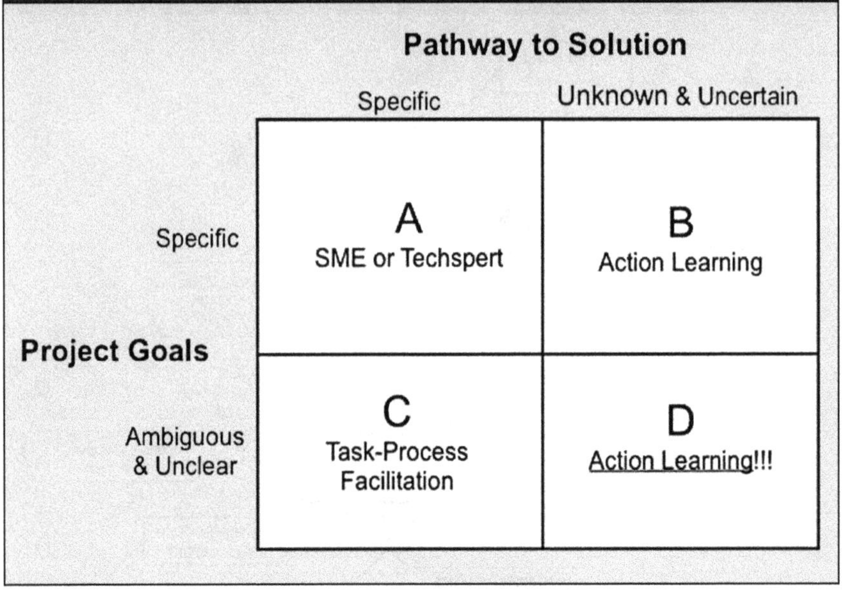

		Pathway to Solution	
		Specific	Unknown & Uncertain
Project Goals	Specific	**A** SME or Techspert	**B** Action Learning
	Ambiguous & Unclear	**C** Task-Process Facilitation	**D** Action Learning!!!

On the other hand, if the project goal is known and specific but the pathway to the solution (i.e., the strategy and action steps) is unknown or uncertain, then action learning is appropriate. The same conclusion is valid when both the goal and the pathway are ambiguous, unclear, unknown, or uncertain. It is critical that you understand and use this matrix in carefully making your staffing and deployment decisions since placing either type of consultant in a wrong quadrant will only create frustration and confusion.

CHAPTER 7.

The Compelling Need for Action Learning?

Confusion about Coaching. If you decide that you need consultants who are proficient in action learning team coaching, you are also obliged to consider several of the following factors.

First, there is a large population of people with various kinds of training and certifications that offer *executive coaching* services – that is, one-on-one individual coaching. These coaches often believe and portray themselves as being competent to also coach teams of various kinds. An assessment of the quality of this vast array of people is beyond the scope of this booklet. However, even the best executive coaches are not likely to be competent in coaching a team without comprehensive training. They might be competent in one-to-one coaching, but that skill set does not easily transfer to team coaching.

A related concern is the possibility that an executive coach who has individual sessions with some or all members of an executive management team may be asked to coach the team itself. We believe this violates the psychologists' code of ethical conduct in regard to *dual relationships*. And, at a pragmatic level, how can executive coaches maintain their neutrality during team sessions when they have had multiple confidential coaching sessions with some or all team members?

Second, you must not satisfy yourself when some consultant says, "We do action learning." There are a number of organizational interventions being offered by consultants that are called, "Action Learning." In truth, the term is frequently applied to any planned activity that calls for participants to take some kind of action rather than merely serving as an audience to one or more sages-on-stage. Such variations of experiential training do not qualify as "action learning." Rather, they are active interventions ranging from outward-bound excursions, ropes or obstacle courses, case studies, skill practice exercises, off-site visits, action research projects, and structured and unstructured or self-directed groups that attempt to solve simulated or actual organizational problems.

While there might be some similarities, these activities are limited in scope and are based on substantively different theories, methods, values, skills, applications, and outcomes[1]. The variations that are close to our conception of action learning trace their origins to Reg Revans (e.g., 1998). You or your staff will have to sort through your potential action learning coaches and weed out the false positives. While a detailed comparison of the most frequent variations is beyond the scope of this book, the references in the footnote provide you with some direction for self-study.

Third, and most important, action learning is an elegantly straightforward and powerful, yet disciplined approach for dealing with *radical, unprecedented, transformational changes* that create large, complex organizational problem situations. Consultants who believe they understand complex systemic problems may offer to deliver

---

1. Some examples of different versions of Action Learning are: Boshyk (2002), Coughlan & Coghlan (2011), Dotlich & Noel (1998), Gasparski & Botham (1998), Marquardt, Leonard, Freedman, & Hill (2009), Marquardt (2011), O'Neil & Marsick (2007), Revans (1998), Rothwell (1999), Torbert & associates (2004), and Ulrich, Kerr, & Ashkenas (2002).

pre-structured organizational change interventions; they believe they can use these off-the-shelf strategies and procedures to effectively and efficiently guide organizational members to solve their problems. This may be valid in some instances; however, we would require evidence to support this implicit assumption. As organizational leaders and decision-makers, you will have to discern who has the requisite experiences and competencies.

If you are primarily concerned with just fixing what is broken or improving what is underperforming, SME or techspert consultants might be perfect for you. However, you may want employees at all levels to *both* solve the problem *and* learn how to deal with similar unprecedented, discontinuous problems on their own, develop leadership competencies, learn how to work in participative teams, and develop skills in planning and managing organizational change. If so, you really must consider either starting change initiatives with action learning or blending action learning coaches into a multidisciplinary change project teams along with SMEs, techsperts, trainer-educators, and task or process facilitators. You may have to insist on including action learning coaches since many techspert management consultants do not know about, understand, feel comfortable about adding action learning coaches to their consulting teams, or know where and when to deploy them. And, they may also be reluctant to bring another kind of consultant into a contract with a limited budget.

Understanding action learning. Action learning differs from other apparently similar organizational interventions because of its multiple objectives. As leaders, it is imperative that you make clear what you want and need for an action learning project – not only to other kinds of consultants but also to your employees who are involved as project design and implementation team members or are stakeholders who will be affected by the execution of solutions. You must continuously point out that there are at least four outcomes of an action learning project, as shown in Figure 7.1. That is, participants will develop recommendations for solutions while acquiring knowledge and skills in problem solving, personal and leadership development, team development, and organizational change.

You will find it useful to use Figure 7.1 to explain to various involved parties that the source of these outcomes is expressed in the action learning formula: L = P x Q x R. That is, *Learning* (L) is a function of *Programmed Knowledge* (P) x *Questions* (Q) or inquiry x *Reflection* (R).

Figure 7.1. The Four Outcomes of Action Learning

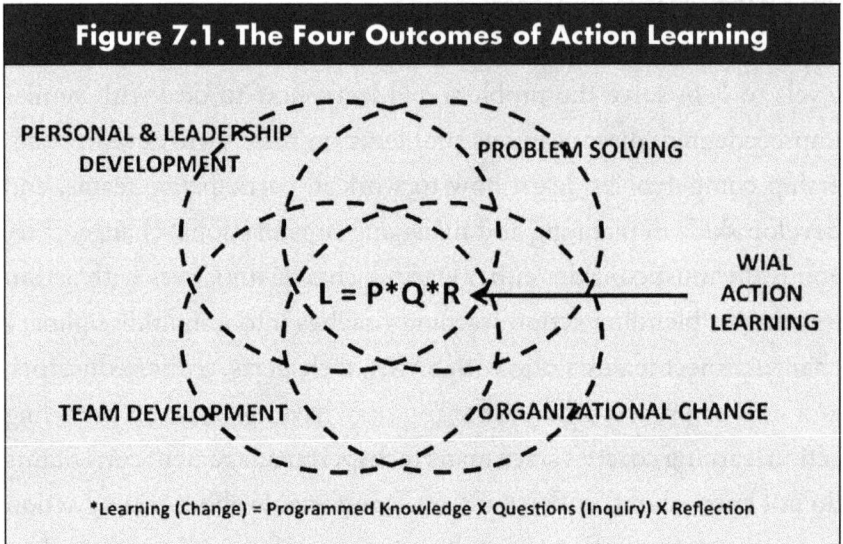

PERSONAL & LEADERSHIP DEVELOPMENT

PROBLEM SOLVING

$L = P*Q*R$

WIAL ACTION LEARNING

TEAM DEVELOPMENT

ORGANIZATIONAL CHANGE

*Learning (Change) = Programmed Knowledge X Questions (Inquiry) X Reflection

Reg Revans (1998) believed that learning is a function of "P" (programmed knowledge) plus "Q" (questions or inquiry). Mike Marquardt (1999, 2011) added "R" (reflection) to the formula. With their focus on inquiry and reflection, action learning coaches enable team members to learn how to learn from their collective experience with solving real problems.

At every opportunity that you can create to reach employees and stakeholders, you should emphasize that the experience of participating in action learning enables team members to practice and enhance their competence, confidence, and comfort with applying the values, principles, knowledge, skills, and aptitudes that comprise the discipline of action learning in addition to earning satisfaction from solving critical problems. You can point out that team members will also experiment, make mistakes, and develop and learn to apply these competencies effectively within and beyond the action learning team. Thereby, they will contribute to solving problems and increasing the effectiveness of the larger organization and its interdependent subsystems. Thus, the benefits have the potential to spread far beyond the boundaries of the action learning team.

Other interventions that may be called Action Learning but do not employ inquiry and reflection focus primarily on "P" – that is, on pedagogical or arcane theory and knowledge. That narrows and restricts team members' attention to applying only specific subject matter that the consultants believe are related to the problem. Many such approaches are prescriptive, intended to enable team members to avoid making mistakes or wasting time. Often, there is no common sharing of what participants might have learned. So, team members' learnings are likely to be individualized and idiosyncratic. What any given member learns may be different and incomplete relative to others. Action learning team members create comprehensive learnings when they share, discuss, and analyze their individual and collective experiences.

Additionally, in your staff meetings and brown bag lunches or walk-abouts, you can emphasize that in action learning, team members learn about and develop their leadership potential from identifying and working to develop specific behaviors they believe will enhance their leadership and interpersonal competencies. Within their teams, they publicly declare their intention to develop specific leadership or inter-personal behavioral skills and ask fellow team members to help them by observing them during their team sessions and then providing them with feedback – usually at the end of each action learning session. You can encourage each individual team member to take the risk of disclosing their apparent weaknesses (or developmental challenges) and asking for critical, helpful feedback from other team members. This also helps team members to make explicit their assumptions about the problems, themselves, teamwork, and their organization so they can be challenged and tested for validity.

Action learning teams quickly recognize that they cannot operate effectively in isolation. They come to realize that their members do not possess all of the pertinent information they need to clarify and analyze problems and to make informed decisions. They discover that organizational subsystems really are interdependent and that they need to establish and maintain two-way and three-way communications with other subsystems and other hierarchical levels to obtain and disclose essential information. They discover also that people in different parts and levels of the organization have different, often competing interests in how they define the problem, which goals are selected, and which strategy and solution is created. In many cases, stakeholder groups reject efforts to collaborate, excusing themselves by saying they are too busy with their own work to meet with action learning tem members. When you become aware of this, you must take action personally or assure that your associates take action to make sufficient time to remove obstacles and open the avenues for action learning team members to exchange critical information with stakeholders. This also suggests that you must create some proactive process or mechanism to seek and organize such information.

All of that information must be gathered and organized by the action learning team as it reviews and, consequently, modifies its understanding of the problem, as well as their desired states or goals, strategies, and action plans for solutions. Action learning team members also learn that stakeholders must be kept informed of the team's progress and current understanding of the problem. Further, they come to realize they need to be informed of the stakeholders' changing positions, interests, opinions, and preferences as the implementation plan is executed.

For stakeholders to feel committed to supporting the implementation of the team's decisions, you must make sure that they feel their opinions are valued by the action learning team and that they have been actively involved in making these decisions. Two-way and three-way communications – up, down, and sideways – assure a considerable measure of active participation in the action learning team's deliberations. Thus, you can remind team members that they can enhance their capacity for obtaining and utilizing relevant information in a timely manner from diverse sources while activating their stakeholders' emotional investment in and commitment to the enterprise. Action learning teams typically facilitate this information exchange by authorizing their members to function as *envoys* that reach out proactively, connect with stakeholders, provide them with information and obtain their reactions and opinions, bring that information back to the team, and make sure the team uses the information and that the stakeholders know the team has used their input. The enriched variety and amount of information from varied pertinent perspectives improve the quality and viability of the team's decisions and plans.

As a result of engaging and exchanging information with relevant involved subsystems and stakeholders, action learning team members generally establish and maintain trusting relations with members in various parts and levels of their organization. These are people with whom they probably would not have had any contact otherwise. These contacts become critical elements of the social networks that invariable prove valuable beyond the action learning experience.

In the final analysis, action learning team members have the potential to contribute to the creation of an organizational culture that supports taking risks, reducing fear, tolerating mistakes, encouraging experimentation, and continuous learning.

You must indicate clearly that you want and need team members to reach each of the four outcomes before deciding to use action learning as a tool. You want your direct reports and other colleagues to send the same message. Again, if you are primarily concerned only with simply solving obvious problems, you will likely decide that action learning is not necessary and/or unworkable. Using SMEs or techsperts to solve the problems or using task or process facilitators to guide team members through a preconceived, structured problem-solving process (like that of Kepner & Tregoe, 1997) may be more expedient, less time-consuming, less complicated, and probably less expensive. However, these options may prove to be less flexible or adaptive and/or effective than what is needed.

Now that you have explored the question of how many of which kinds of consultants you need for your complex systems change, please consider Part II in which we describe the requisite infrastructure and processes needed to support an organizational change project that involves the deployment of action learning teams. Your active involvement and participation in this review is critical.

PART II.
ACTION LEARNING TEAM PROJECTS

Action Learning – Action learning is an elegantly simple *process* that requires great discipline. Small four to eight person teams (Reg Revans originally called this a "set") work on real, current, urgent, critical, complex, unprecedented organizational problems that team members care about. As we have implied, problems related to small, incremental changes would not be appropriate problems for action learning. These should be dealt with as part of routine managerial operations. Action learning is also not appropriate for moderately complex problems. These should be delegated to task force teams composed of people who work close to the site of the problem, perhaps with the assistance of a techspert or SME consultant.

As part of the action learning process, teams take action to engage and exchange vital information with all involved parties and stakeholders that are affected by the changes and problems, analyze and reflect on the implications of the results of those engagements, develop potential solutions, and learn from the experience. As such, action learning is a powerful management *tool* that creates dynamic opportunities for individuals, teams, leaders, and organizations to learn to successfully adapt and innovate as they meet the challenges of multiple, often simultaneous, significant, transformational, discontinuous changes in their environment.

The action learning team's dual objectives are to both *solve the problems* that are presented to it and to *learn from the experience*. The learning focuses on developing team members' self-awareness, individual leadership and interpersonal skills, participative team problem-solving and decision-making skills, as well as skills in studying and intervening in intergroup and organizational systems dynamics.

When Action Learning Should Be Used. In general, you will want to mobilize and deploy action learning teams (with coaches) whenever your organization or its subsystems are confronted by critical, important, complex, unprecedented problem situations. These problem situations will be challenging if you and your managers do not have viable methods for finding or creating enduring solutions for these challenging situations. You, your managers, and your stakeholders must care a great deal about this problem situation and want it solved. You must also want to learn how to solve similarly unprecedented problem situations in the future.

As part of your complex organizational systems change initiatives, you will discover that you and your colleagues will not have anticipated every possible problem that might occur during (or because of) the implementation of your plan for complex systems change. This is because, paraphrasing Kurt Lewin, *the best way to fully understand an organization is to try to change it*. No change implementation plan that we know of has ever been executed precisely as intended. This is because unexpected and unplanned-for "exceptions" invariably disrupt schedules and budgets. Therefore, you will want to create the capacity to mobilize and deploy action learning teams (with coaches) whenever the change project encounters inevitable unanticipated consequences of changing the system. This will require you to maintain a cadre of potential action learning team members and coaches in anticipation of the occurrence of predictable surprises. By predictable surprises we refer to those unanticipated side effects and consequences of implementing your complex systems change plan. We may not be able to predict what these specific surprises will be but we know, with certainty, that we will be surprised by something. For example, unexpected resistance from a stakeholder that you had assumed would be a supporter of the change. Since contingencies are rarely considered and slack resources like time, budget, and skilled personnel are rarely included in plans for change it will be important for you to develop the systemic capacity to solve these inescapable problems quickly and effectively while also learning from the experiences.

As part of your organization's leadership development program, you will want to use action learning to both solve challenging problems and enable your high potential managers to learn how to learn from their experience. The areas that you will want your potential leaders to learn are self-awareness, interpersonal and leadership skills, collaborating with diverse members of temporary teams to solve urgent and complex problems, proficiency in developing high performance teamwork, ability to deal effectively with problems that occur within and between interdependent subsystems, and capacity to contribute to planning and implementing complex systems change, including predictable surprises.

The Six Elements of Effective Action Learning. Marquardt (1999) described six distinct, albeit interactive, elements that comprise the essential foundation for effective action learning. These are:

1. A compelling, important, urgent, complex, unprecedented problem

2. The action learning team

3. The questioning and reflection process

4. The commitment to taking action

5. The commitment to learning

6. The action learning team coach

As a leader, you might serve as an advisory committee member, champion, or sponsor. In each of these roles you must support the need for maintaining the integrity of all six elements – visibly, consistently, and persistently – in every staff meeting or public event in which you participate; a single e-mail blast simply will not do. Over time, the demands of routine and extraordinary responsibilities are likely to erode the involved parties' commitment to maintain these six elements. Various stakeholders might appeal for lower standards to make it easier to appear to comply with the essential requirements for effective action learning projects. It is your responsibility to resist such influences and hold involved parties accountable for preserving all the elements and keeping intact the commitments of the parties.

Accordingly, it is critical for you and the involved parties to fully understand each of the elements and their implications. Toward that end, the six elements are presented in detail in the following chapters.

CHAPTER 8.

A Compelling Problem

The first element of an action learning project is a compelling, important, urgent, complex, unprecedented problem. That is, it must be compelling for the members of the action learning team. It must capture their attention, imagination, and enthusiasm. They must care about the problem and about finding or creating a viable solution. It must be evident that the problem is important for team members, their back-home subsystems, and the organization as a whole. It must be apparent that solving the problem would make a significant difference in their organization's health and operations. The team must share a sense of urgency in finding or creating a solution swiftly and putting it in place quickly. It must be complex in that the problem must impact several subsystems and hierarchical levels and their respective interactions, regardless of the origin of the problem.

Most complex problems have a primary impact site that may be a single subsystem or a pair or trio of subsystems and their interdependent interactions. In addition, complex problems typically create secondary and tertiary reverberations throughout the organizational system. The compelling, important, urgent, complex problem is also probably unprecedented. That is, it is discontinuous with your organization's past experiences. It is highly probable that your organization has developed its own methods and procedures for solving known problems that deal with incremental and moderately disruptive changes. However, you and your employees will quickly discover that these methods and procedures will not be effective in producing sustainable results when you are dealing with radical, transformational problems. Action learning is an ideal tool to apply to these kinds of problems.

When you choose to use action learning by itself or in conjunction with a larger organizational change project or leadership development program, it is essential that you keep the dual purposes of action learning in mind. The first purpose is that action learning is used to solve discontinuous problems. Secondly, action learning enables team members to learn. These purposes are of equal importance.

Your persistent, visible, public attention to both purposes is critical. Otherwise, your people will naturally focus on the single-loop process of simply solving the problem and neglect the double- and triple-loop processes of learning at the individual, team, and organizational levels. It is imperative that you ensure that champions, sponsors, coaches, and the managers of team members will persistently keep the attention of action learning team members and their stakeholders firmly fixed equally on both purposes.

Task or process facilitation emphasizes solving problems with the facilitator providing instructions and guiding a team through a predetermined process. Learning occurs at the individual level but this is likely to be idiosyncratic. That is, team members do not explicitly discuss and share what they have learned with each other so they do not create comprehensive, inclusive team learnings that can be archived and contribute to continuous organizational learning. Individuals often leave the process with many different unshared, unexamined perspectives. Some of these might prove useful; many others do not. Team members do not learn what others have learned. Whatever valuable lessons might have been learned are not systematically collected, archived, or routinely passed on to the rest of the organization.

On the other hand, training or educational interventions empha-size learning predetermined subject matter – e.g., theory, research results, methods, procedures, or skills – rather than learning from personal experience while solving real problems. Training and educa-tional interventions mostly use lectures, films, and artificial, contrived case studies, simulations, or skill development exercises that have a single correct solution; in fact, the materials they present are more like puzzles than real-life problems.

Action learning requires that executives, champions, and sponsors assign real-life, current organizational problems to their action learn-ing teams. The many factors that contribute to these problems will not have been known in the beginning. They will not have a predetermined correct solution. The desired state might be vague and uncertain. Accordingly, the solutions that teams create and recommend cannot be predicted in the beginning.

You might have to direct subordinate executives, champions, and/ or sponsors to identify and specify a serious organizational problem for each action learning team. The same problem is not to be assigned to more than a single team.

Three Problematic Conditions and Two Classes of Problems. The notion of a "problem" is bi-modal. From the perspective of action learning, there are two classes of problems. First, there is the *current state* of the organizational system or some part or aspect of the system. The current state might include any one or any combination of three problematic conditions.

1. One or more interdependent elements of the organizational system might be *broken* or is *underperforming*. For example, coordination among subsystems that comprise the organiza-tion's delivery chain has deteriorated. Dissatisfaction arises

from down time and inefficiencies when involved parties expect and need uninterrupted, smooth running operations.

2. An *opportunity* to improve effectiveness and add value to the organization might be discovered. For example, a new market for the organization's existing goods or services has opened up. Dissatisfaction arises from the frustrations that involved parties experience when they realize they are not taking quick advantage of these opportunities and, therefore, are likely to lose business to their competitors.

3. Efforts to permanently fix what appeared to be something that was broken might have worked for a brief period of time but then reappeared in the same or a somewhat different form People realize they are dealing with a *dilemma*. For example, it might become apparent that certain centralized organizational functions had more disadvantages than benefits. These functions were, therefore, decentralized. This resulted in enhanced benefits and improved performance for a short time. But then, the disadvantages of decentralization became apparent, so the functions were centralized once again. And the cycle continued. Dissatisfaction arises from the disappointments that involved parties experience as they realize that permanent solutions cannot be found or created and applied to these perpetual and ongoing dilemmas.

Each of the conditions described above generates *dissatisfaction*. This emotion constitutes the *energy* that drives individual and organizational efforts to find or create effective, enduring solutions. Broken or underperforming elements must be fixed to optimize the organization's performance. Opportunities must be capitalized upon or exploited to contribute to the organization's growth. While it may not be possible to solve dilemmas permanently, they must be managed to avoid periodic but predictable emergencies that waste organization resources.

The second class of problem is revealed by considering the question, *"What solution might the action learning team find or create that will close the gap between the current state (the 'problem') and the desired state (the 'goal')?"* No matter whether the current problem situation is something that is broken or underperforming, an unexploited opportunity, or an unmanaged dilemma, the basic, most fundamental problem is always *how to close the gap between the current dissatisfying state and the desired state or goal* (see Figure 8.1).

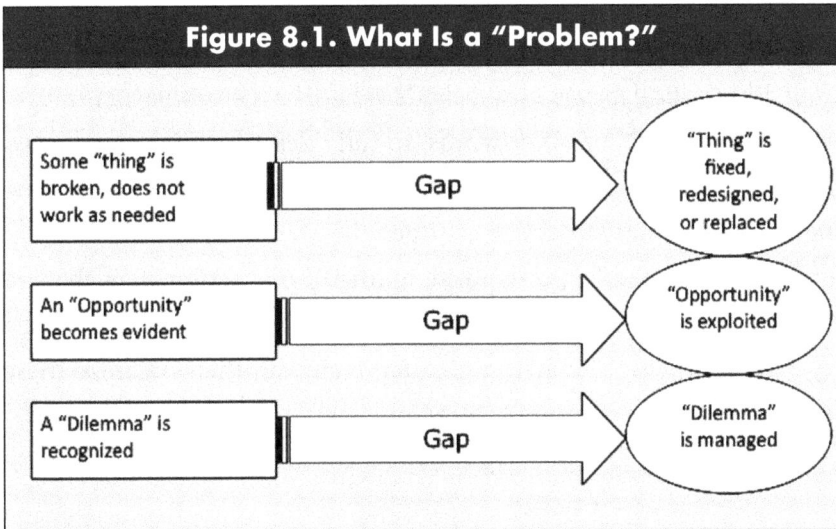

Figure 8.1. What Is a "Problem?"

This second class of problem also requires the action learning team to specify and analyze the multiplicity of forces that operate within the system that either *drive* the organization in the direction of the goal or *obstruct* efforts to move in that positive, desired direction. Teams are frequently tempted to find a single cause of and a single solution for problems, but they will eventually discover that problems are generally *over-determined*, i.e., a single problem is caused by a number of contributing root cause factors. The implicit assumption that there must be a single cause is widespread but simplistic. Assumptions like this must be surfaced and tested for their validity *and* disproved. There is not a single reason why the organization is or is not moving toward the goal. Rather, as a result of a thorough problem analysis, teams discover multiple driving and many restraining forces.

You, in concert with the champion, sponsors, and action learning coaches must encourage the action learning teams to persist until they have uncovered at least the most important three or four of these drives and restraints. Otherwise, the teams are likely to satisfy themselves with the first drive or restraint that they come across. If this occurs, the teams' effectiveness will be sharply diminished because they will have misled themselves. Action learning coaches might ask, *"OK, you have identified one factor that makes it difficult to achieve the goal. Now, what other critical factors are involved? What else is operating in the organizational system?"* In other words, to fully describe this second class of problem, the action learning team must identify the various driving and restraining forces that are operating in the system. This kind of analysis is an essential prerequisite to identifying action steps that are likely to either enhance the driving forces or reduce or eliminate the restraining forces. The action learning team can then organize these action steps into a comprehensive implementation plan or solution.

CHAPTER 9.

The Action Learning Team

Action learning teams are deliberately small. They are composed of four to eight members. Members are intentionally selected for their *diversity* – for example, education, occupation, organizational role and function, tenure, level in the organization's hierarchy, technical training and experience, and, perhaps, native language, nationality, gender, and race.

These teams are also *temporary*, as they disband after their recommended solutions are approved and implemented. However, we recommend that at least some members of the action learning team be deployed as members of the implementation project. This provides continuity and serves to instill in the implementation project at least some of the emotional investment and commitment that the action learning team developed.

Ideally, at least one team member should be a critical thinking, intelligent person who is *ignorant* of the nature of the causes of the change and the problems the changes create (the better to ask great naïve questions that more informed members are usually reluctant to ask).

That person is often called, *"the pizza person[2]."* Team members may or may not have first-hand familiarity with the problem situation and the subsystems and people who are directly and indirectly involved. The teams may also choose to include stakeholders and external resources, i.e., SMEs and/or techsperts, from time to time, as needed, as *temporary* or auxiliary team members.

There are a number of ways to build action learning teams. Action learning team members may be recruited as volunteers or assigned to serve. In one organization, for example, a half-day orientation to action learning was conducted to both explain and demonstrate the fundamentals of action learning. The orientation was open to all employees; over 50 people participated. At the conclusion, the CEO presented four problems – one for each of four teams – and asked for volunteers to serve as action learning team members. Thirty-four people volunteered. Since the organization wanted four teams of six people, a team of four executives (who would be sponsors) selected 24 of the volunteers. The sponsors decided which of the selected volunteers would be assigned to which action learning team.

One criterion for making assignments was that team members should come from different subsystems or work units that were directly or indirectly involved with or affected by the problem situation (see Figure 9.1). Another criterion was that different levels of the organizational hierarchy should be represented on each team. A third was that prospective team members should have different technical education, training, or experience. As it happened, these criteria also served to

---

2. Based on a story told by Mike Marquardt in which a government agency action learning team worked late one night and ordered out for pizza. The delivery man came, looked around the meeting room and began asking about the contents of the newsprint charts that were posted all over the walls. Most team members wanted the pizza person to leave, but Mike asked him to stay to ask more naïve questions. I guess they paid him for his time. After a while, he asked why there were so many interconnected action steps and why couldn't they skip from step 4 directly to step 7. The team discussed the proposal and, finally, agreed. Mike swears the pizza person saved the government agency 35 million dollars.

engage prospective team members who varied by gender, nationality, and race. But the sponsors could have used these characteristics as explicit selection criteria.

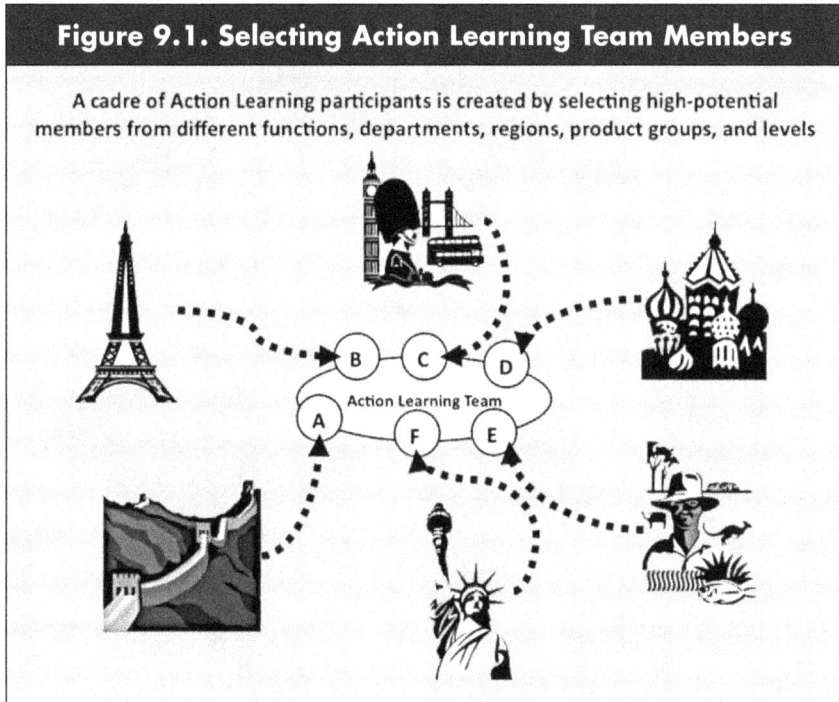

Figure 9.1. Selecting Action Learning Team Members

A cadre of Action Learning participants is created by selecting high-potential members from different functions, departments, regions, product groups, and levels

In addition, each team member should be committed to both solving the problem as well as to learning. Each should have a stake in the problem and its solution, except, perhaps, for the pizza person.

You should be aware that any problem situation will be perceived differently by people at different levels, subsystems, or work units in an organization. When compared with solutions generated by a homogeneous population – e.g., all accountants – sharing these varied perceptions generally result in a more comprehensive definition of the problem situation and its significance. However, for some, a given problem situation will represent a potential threat, while others will perceive potential advantages in the same problem situation and its solution. The threats and advantages will vary from subsystem to subsystem; the meanings and significance that team members attribute to the problem situation also will be different.

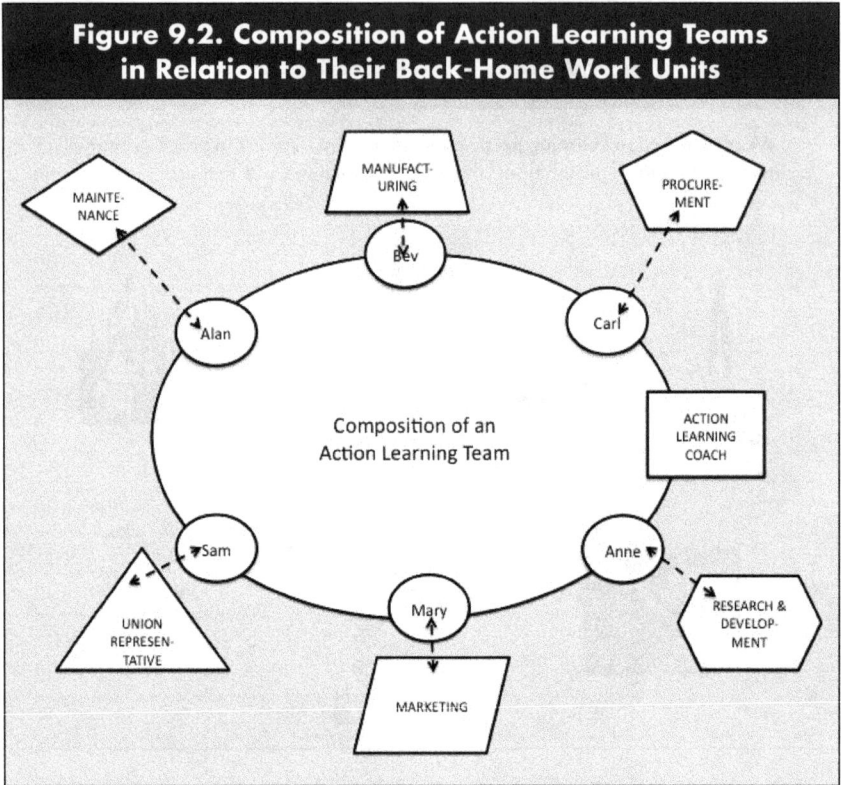

Figure 9.2. Composition of Action Learning Teams in Relation to Their Back-Home Work Units

Team members generally see themselves as unofficial representatives of their home work units and believe that they have to protect the *interests* of those subsystems. You should expect various team members to take contrary positions during team analyses and decisions; they will compete with one another to satisfy what they believe those interests are. As such, it is very important for action learning coaches to help their teams get beyond individual team members' *positions* so that the basic interests of their respective home subsystems can surface and be discussed openly and explicitly. In this way, more realistic and useful information will be revealed about the context within which the problem situation exists.

Teams must be prepared to deal with the apparent dilemma that each of its member may face: Either satisfy their respective back-home systems' interests and sacrifice the interests of their larger organizational system or sacrifice the interests of their back-home subsystems and satisfy the needs of their larger organizational system. Explicitly recognizing and discussing the advantages and disadvan-tages of both sides of this either-or dilemma may lead to the discov-ery of some creative means of managing both the interests of team members' home subsystems and the interests of their larger organiza-tional system. Thus, the action learning team may modify their under-standing of the current state, the goal, or the solution – or all three.

Therefore, team members should have sufficient capacity for *critical analysis* to comprehend the problems, opportunities, or dilemmas and their systemic implications. They should be *intuitive* enough to appre-ciate the implications of the given problem for the larger organization – in addition to the implications for themselves and their own business units. They should be capable of becoming familiar with the *context* of the changes and the *derivative* problems. Finally, they should each make action learning sessions a very high priority and feel committed to *attend all action learning meetings.*

Executive Action Required. The commitment to attend all action learning team meetings is critical and, too often, generates the prob-lem of irregular and changing membership of the teams. Key people and their intellectual resources are missing when needed. People who would have acted as emissaries to stakeholder subsystems are not avail-able, so the flow of information between the action learning team and its stakeholder subsystems is interrupted. The team is denied access to current information. And, when missing members do show up, scarce team time is consumed in bringing tardy or absentee team members up to date.

Problems like these are caused when the managers or supervisors of action learning team members fail to provide adequate *release time* so they can attend meetings and perform other required action learning team functions between sessions. This creates a double burden for action learning team members: they must perform their exceptional action learning team responsibilities in *addition* to their routine work unit responsibilities.

The best and the brightest people are usually selected or volunteer for action learning teams, but they are often so overworked that they either come late or leave early or miss team sessions entirely so they can get their routine work done. Faced with a choice between meeting their managers' expectations and fulfilling their obligations to their action learning teams, most team members often focus on satisfying their managers. They are acutely aware that they are evaluated by their managers for their performance of routine work *and not for their performance in their action learning teams.* This problem is exacerbated when the performance management systems for the team members' managers exclude a measure of their active support of their subordinate action learning team members. This also represents a failure of the managers' bosses to emphasize the importance of their active support, to hold the managers accountable, and to create meaningful consequences for positive actions or lack thereof. More important, though, is that you must initiate negotiations with human resource management personnel to restructure managers' performance appraisals to include measures of this kind of support. For example, when action learning team members are deployed on action learning team business, their managers would use the absences as opportunities to delegate the team members' routine responsibilities to other employees. These would be developmental learning opportunities for those persons. Everyone would gain. Managerial support includes identifying and removing obstacles and impediments to team members' activities and authorizing or initiating contacts between action learning team members and relevant involved subsystems and stakeholders. In addition, you must make sure there is good faith negotiating with human resource management in modifying the performance management systems for action learning team members to include an assessment of the team members' performance in their action learning teams.

CHAPTER 10.

Inquiry: The Questioning and Reflection Process

You might find that some other executives, managers, or team members will complain to you when they first experience their action learning coaches in action. The complaints tend to occur when team members discover that their action learning coach only asks questions rather than acting in the far more familiar roles that are performed by task facilitators or techspert consultants. (These consultants probably have provided comforting structure and guidance to clients in the past.)

In order to convince critics to suspend their disbelief, you must be convinced that inquiry and reflection will result in innovative and effective solutions[3]. Otherwise, you will not be able to provide organizational members with the firm assurances they need to take the risk of supporting action learning, the teams, and their members.

Accordingly, what follows is essential for you to fully understand, accept, and believe in the fundamental importance of inquiry.

Inquiry – This consists of the "great" questions that cause team members to pause and reflect and which drive the elegant,

_____

3.   To gain some insight into the significance of asking great questions, see: Adams, 2009; Browne & Keeley, 2007; Marquardt, 2005; or Vogt, Brown, & Isaacs, 2003.

straightforward methodology of action learning. This becomes evident as action learning team members follow the two ground rules of action learning:

First: *Statements are made only in response to questions. Anyone in the action learning team can ask anyone else a question at any time.*

The first ground rule is supported by the second: *The action learning coach is authorized to intervene whenever there is an opportunity for learning. The coach also keeps track of time.*

However, simply making sure that team members ask some kind of question to begin a dialog is inadequate. People for whom problem-solving is their primary function seem to be predisposed to ask leading questions that can be answered yes-or-no or where the respondent is offered a multiple choice question that can be answered by choosing either the "A" or "B" option. Contrariwise, open-ended questions help action learning team members to clarify both the current situation and the goal or desired state.

Open-ended questions encourage team members to say whatever they are thinking, very often tapping into their preconscious thinking – i.e., thoughts of which they are not consciously aware but can easily be accessed when asked the right question (for example, the answer to the question, *"In what town did you grow up?"* would probably not be a conscious thought during a business meeting, but, if and when asked, you can easily access and retrieve the answer from your pre-conscious). Team members would probably not express a preconscious thought if they were asked a leading (yes/no or multiple choice) question; they would simply focus on the options presented.

The most useful information is elicited when action learning team members learn to *ask open-ended questions for which they do not have answers* and that take *courage* to ask and are *difficult* to answer.

Open-ended questions create opportunities for deep reflection and allow team members to share their feelings about a problem situation and its implications. Such questions also compel team members to focus, listen, and reflect. They encourage team members and problem presenters to elaborate, stretch beyond conventional thinking, and open up new avenues and insights that lead to new and deeper exploration, making implicit assumptions explicit and make it possible to test their validity. Open-ended questions also tend to create a systems perspective of the problem situation, and challenge team members to be creative, to examine cause and effect relationships rather than merely surface symptoms of a set of root causes, and to learn. Open-ended questions can also create the time and space that members need to pause, reflect, scan and retrieve relevant information from their pre-conscious, and to gain new perspectives.

The power of questions to lead to break-through thinking that, in turn, leads to creative solutions is based on three hypotheses:

1. It is not possible to find great solutions to difficult problems without significant *learning*;

2. It is not possible to learn deeply without *reflecting*; and

3. It is not possible to reflect without a *question* (based on Marquardt, 2011).

When problem presenters are asked the open-ended question, *"What is the problem that you want the team to help you with?"* they usually respond in one of two ways. First, problem presenters frequently say something like, *"Well, my employees are* not *performing the way we need them to perform."* Alternatively, they might say, *"We don't know how to create our desired state (or reach our goal)."* In either case, the task of the action learning team is to ask the presenter great questions to help him or her clarify both the problem situation and the goal. The action learning coach helps team members ask unbiased and powerful open-ended questions by using his or her questions to either *model* the proper form of questions or to *shape* the team members' questions so they take the proper form and make an effective impact.

In the first case, the action learning team members might not recognize that the problem statement is actually a negative description of some aspect of the presenter's solution or desired state. This is clearly seen when you delete the word, *"not."* Then the statement becomes: *"Employees are performing as we need them to perform."* This becomes apparent if the action learning coach models the proper form of questions by asking, *"What happens to that statement when you delete the word, 'not'?"* As team members recognize the distinction between the two versions of similar questions and their significance, other questions suggest themselves.

An uncommon example of a useful question might be, *"If they are not performing as you expect or need, what are your employees doing?"* This is useful because it is both open-ended and invites the problem presenter to consider in detail the nature of the current problem state. It also creates an opportunity to drill down by asking, *"Why are your employees doing that instead of what you need them to do?"* And, *"What are the consequences for your employees not doing what you want?"*

At this stage, good open-ended questions elicit more and more useful information.

Another kind of open-ended question focuses the respondent's attention on clarifying the implicit, ultimate goal. For example, *"Why is it important for employees to perform as expected?"* And, drilling down, *"For whom is it important for your employees to perform as you want?"* (It often happens that performance discrepancies like this occur when the performance is important to management but not to employees (Mager & Pipe, 1999).) These are useful questions because they are also open-ended and they invite the problem presenter to consider the *desirable* consequences of performing as expected. Such questions treat the apparent goal as merely instrumental to achieving something else that the instrumental goal or milestone leads to and is more important. Accordingly, finding a way to induce employees to perform as needed becomes an important part of a solution; however, this is not a goal.

The real goal will become evident when employees perform as needed or the coach asks, *"Why is it important to reach to reach this milestone?"*

A common example of a counterproductive question would be, *"Can you motivate employees by offering them monthly merit increases when they perform as needed?"* This is a close-ended, yes-or-no kind of question that narrows and focuses the presenter's attention on only one of many potential solutions. First of all, it may be premature to start looking for solutions before the current state and the desired future state are fully specified. Further, such questions contain the inquirer's personal theory (e.g., merit increases will motivate employees) and ask the respondent to confirm or reject that theory, rather than create an opportunity for respondents or presenters to disclose what they actually think, without limits.

The action learning coach might help team members to shape this theory-in-the-form-of-a-question into proper form by asking, *"What are you trying to achieve by asking that question?"* Team members usually respond by saying, *"I'm trying to find out what possible solutions the presenter has thought about."* Coaches would follow up by asking, *"How can you ask your question in a way that you get the information you want without suggesting a possible solution?"* In most instances, team members quickly realize they have asked close-ended, yes-or-no questions and rephrase it by asking, *"What solutions have you thought about?"*

In the second case, the problem presenter's problem is of the *"how to"* genre. This kind of problem statement refers to both the goal and to a possible solution that would lead to achieving that goal. Implicitly, the presenter is inviting the team to suggest possible solutions. Without an intervention by the action learning coach or self-correction, teams generally accept the invitation and begin to brainstorm possible action steps or strategies they believe will help presenters to get to their goals.

In jumping to the solution generation phase, teams often neglect to examine and agree upon the definition of the current problem situations or to specifically define the desired states or goals. To avoid this kind of premature action, coaches might model how to focus the team's attention on clarifying the current problem situation so team members learn to ask an open-ended question like, *"For what problem would that be a solution?"* Or, coaches might shape team members' questions so they focus on clarifying the goal or desired state by asking, *"If you take that action, what consequences or results would you expect?"* And then, *"How would this desired state be different from conditions as they currently exist?"* These kinds of questions stimulate team members' willingness to deeply reflect, making it easy to gain clarity and specificity about the nature of the discrepancy between the current problem state and the desired state. By specifying this gap, teams enable themselves to undertake the real problem of analyzing what makes it difficult to move from the current state to the desired state. Based on this analysis the action learning team can then generate ideas about strategies and action steps that would contribute to eliminating or reducing the power of the factors that inhibit or obstruct movement in the direction of the goal.

Learning to ask open-ended questions enables the action learning team to elicit *divergent* perspectives, information, and opinions from its members as well as from representatives of various stakeholder subsystems. This is particularly useful during the initial phases of the problem solving sequence as it provides the team with diverse yet comprehensive information not only about the focal problem but also about the organizational context. In this situation, the analysis of the information might reveal how related interdependent subsystems might have contributed to the causes of the problem as well as to how they might be needed to support and contribute to planning and enacting a viable solution.

The analysis should consider also how the execution of the solution might impact various related organizational subsystems and their interdependent interactions. In such an action-oriented milieu, the team can analyze problems from a systems perspective and consider various options before attitudes *converge* towards narrowing options.

This allows the team to choose optimal strategies and action plans for solutions.

Figure 10.1. The Cycle of Effective Problem Solving

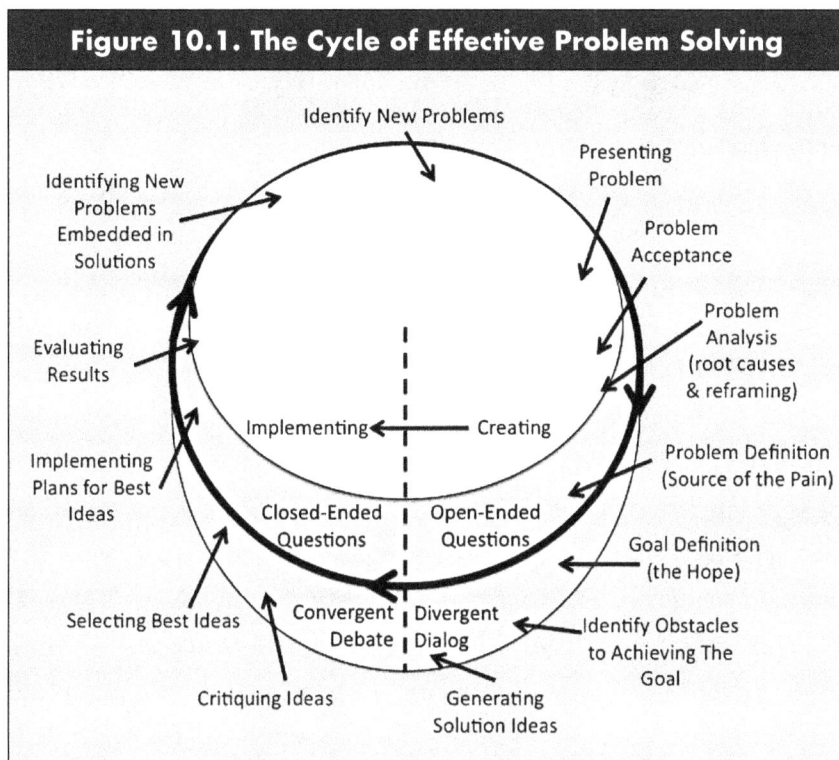

As shown in Figure 10.1, action learning teams enter the convergent phase of their problem solving when they have more or less completed the process of generating solution ideas (i.e., potential action steps) and as they begin to critique and select the best ideas for inclusion into the proposed recommended solution.

At this point, *close-ended questions* are appropriate. Such questions serve the useful purposes of limiting debate and enabling teams to focus on the process of making decisions (e.g., *"Is the team ready to make a decision?"*), determining specific information (e.g., *"When does the committee expect us to present our proposed solution?"*), identify preferences (e.g., *"Do our stakeholders prefer strategy A or Strategy B?"*), helping team members to choose between optional strategies and action steps, thus eliminating tangential or trivial possibilities and focusing on the more viable and effective elements of a solution.

As options are reduced and firm decisions are made, team members use close-ended questions to move toward near-consensus in completing their tasks and bringing issues to closure as they finalize their proposed solutions.

Nonetheless, open-ended questions might prove to be useful at any phase of the problem-solving process. For example, as they prepare presentations of their recommendations, action learning teams sometimes fail to apply critical thinking to some very practical issues. If team members have not already addressed these issues, action learning coaches might model or shape team members' more open-ended questions in which your organizational decision-makers are likely to be very interested. Thus, they are apt to ask such questions as: *"What are the criteria that you, the decision-makers, will use to determine if a proposed solution is acceptable?"* *"Why might the decision-makers reject this proposed solution?"* Or, *"Why might this proposed solution fail?"* And, drilling deeper for greater specificity, the team's reflection might lead to more explicit questions such as *"To what extent will the value of the results of this recommended solution be greater than the likely monetary, opportunity, and psychological costs?"* Or, *"How can we determine if the organization has sufficient resources to support the imple-mentation of the recommendation?"*

CHAPTER 11.

Commitment to Taking Action Throughout the Action Learning Process

You need to understand the specific steps involved in the action learning project process. Indeed, knowledge of the tasks and activities that comprise each step can help all of the participants on the action team visualize both their roles and responsibilities regarding the action learning process.

This chapter is meant to define which involved team member should take responsibility for performing each task or activity or for making sure that each activity is performed by an appropriate designated person.

To understand where, when, and with whom the various members, you included, must or should take action, it is essential for all participants to first understand and agree with the steps to be taken throughout the process of implementing an action learning project.

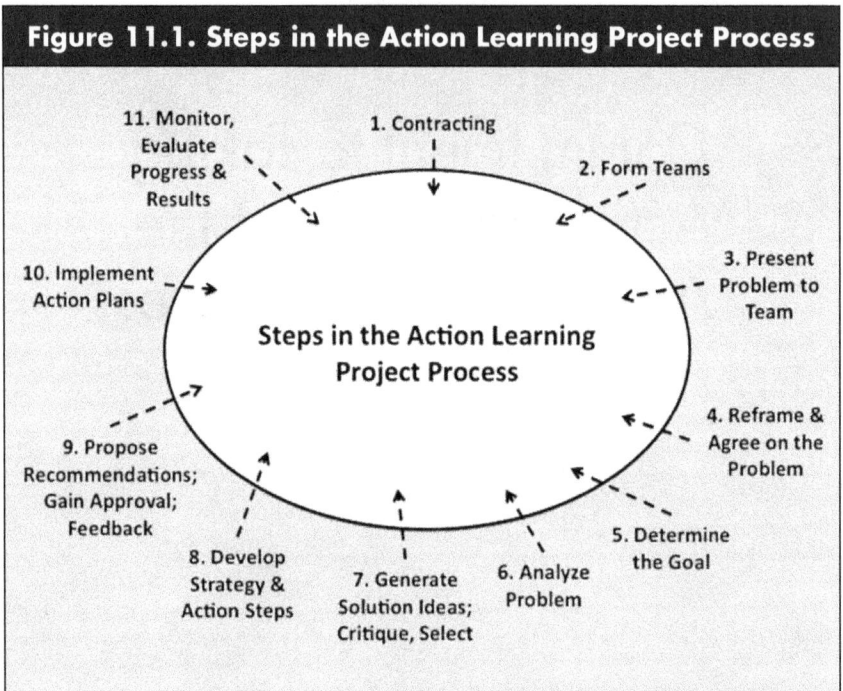

Figure 11.1. Steps in the Action Learning Project Process

Whether you authorize a single action learning team to recommend a solution for a single problem or a number of action learning teams that can develop solutions for a list of problems matters little. To succeed, each team should strive to follow the same sequence of activities outlined below.

1. *Contracting: Establishing a Comprehensive Action Learning Project Structure.* This is the first and most critical element that must be in place to assure an effective action learning project. In general, consulting contracts should include: (1) a description of services to be provided by the consultant; (2) a description of responsibilities to be assumed by the client organization; (3) payment for services; (4) term of engagement; (5) termination contingencies; (6) confidentiality; (7) indemnification of provider; (8) limitations of agreement; (9) severability; and (10) applicable law. [Note: It is important that contracts are

negotiated, written, and signed before the initial orientation session.]

A contract with action learning coaches may stand alone, as in situations where action learning is the initial effort in a larger organizational change or leadership development effort. However, you might develop contracts with several other kinds of consultants to provide a leadership development program or an organizational change initiative where action learning is a sub-contract. All contracts should be negotiated to the mutual satisfaction of both the organization and the consultants and, where appropriate, sub-contractors – such as action learning coaches.

You are responsible for making sure that the following elements are included in the contract for action learning services. These contract elements define the functions shown in Figure 11.1. In addition, the activities that define each phase in the cycle of effective problem solving are shown in Figure 11.2. Therefore, you and your subordinate managers will:

a. Design and conduct an orientation meeting for all action learning team members, sponsors, champions, advisory committee members, executive management team members, and managers of prospective team members. The agenda for the session should include a brief description of action learning, the infrastructure of the project, introductions of key persons, a demonstration by an action learning team developing plans for selecting members for each action learning team and for assigning a problem to each team.

b. Provide a different current, critical, urgent, complex, unprecedented organizational *problem* for each action learning team – a problem for which no known organizational solution exists.

c.   Determine whether or not a steering committee is necessary as a means of engaging representatives of the larger organization and significant stakeholders. The steering committee would collect and provide the project with information from various parts and levels of the organization about the expected and unexpected effects of the planning and implementation of the change initiative. In turn, the steering committee would receive information about progress from the project management team for dissemination to the members of the various stakeholder groups.

d.   Assign one senior executive to serve as the *champion* of the action learning project – if there are multiple action learning teams in operation. Champions will be the liaison between executive management and the action learning team sponsors. They will be responsible for removing policy, procedural, structural, or practice obstacles that impede the activities of the action learning team. They will ensure that critical information is exchanged among various involved subsystems. They might also deal with any operational or logistical problems that emerge during the life of the action learning project, for example, negotiating team members' release time from their routine responsibilities.

e.   One senior manager will serve as a *sponsor* for each action learning team. The sponsor will present the designated problem and then will be available throughout the lifetime of the action learning team as a liaison between the action learning team and the champion or executive management.

Sponsors will also be primarily responsible for negotiating release time for action learning team members with those members' supervisors.

f. Recruit and form teams of four to eight volunteers or appointed team members from relevant subsystems and organizational levels. Relevance is based on the proximity of the team members' subsystems to the causes of the change and the subsequent problems that might arise when subsystems are affected either by the causes or subsequent problems.

g. Hire one fully qualified and certified action learning team coach for each team. The only institute that certifies action learning coaches is the World Institute for Action Learning or WIAL (see www.wial.org).

h. For projects with more than four action learning teams, hire an experienced program manager who is familiar and comfortable with action learning projects and action learning coaches. The program manager will manage logistics and monitor progress, identify emerging unexpected consequences, side effects, and predictable surprises, and liaise with sponsors and the champion.

i. Ensure that agreements are negotiated with the human resources department and the managers of the action learning team members, to modify the performance appraisal system to ensure that team members have release time to participate in the action learning team without having to simultaneously continue their routine employment responsibilities. Also, team members' performance appraisals must be modified to include their performance on the action learning teams.

j.   Ensure that each action learning team meets on a scheduled basis for the designated period of time in a meeting room equipped with a computer-projector, poster charts with markers and tape, round tables, and comfortable chairs for team members, a coach, and two additional temporary visitors.

You are also responsible for creating consequences – both positive and negative – for people to whom various responsibilities are delegated.

The managers of the action learning team members must be included in the action learning project structure, as they might become facilitating assets or obstacles during the lifetime of the project. Figure 11.2 illustrates the roles involved in the temporary structure of a large action learning project.

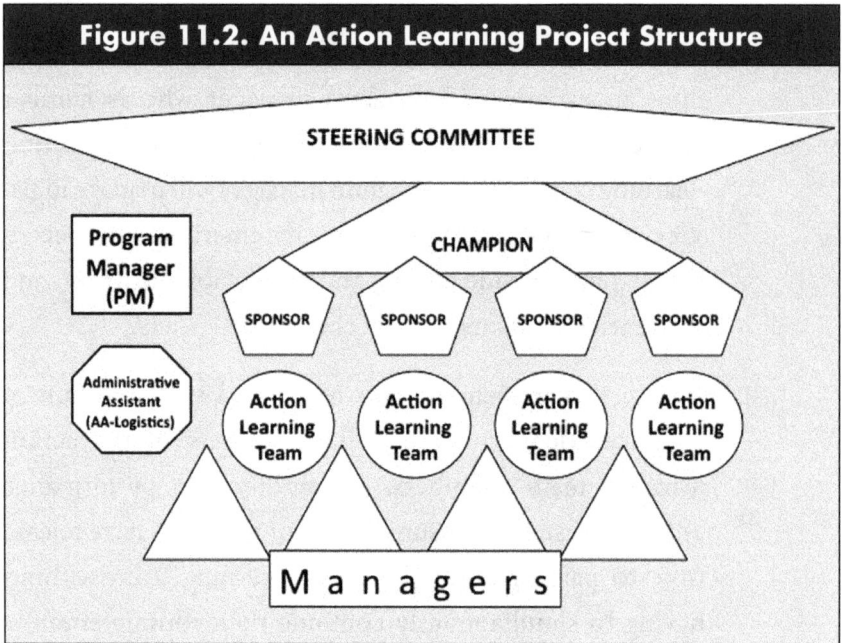

Figure 11.2. An Action Learning Project Structure

1. *Form Team(s).* One team is needed for each identified problem. The same problem must not be assigned to two teams.

2. *Present Problems to Teams.* Sponsors, as problem presenters, might remain with the action learning team for an hour or so after presenting the problem. They can then respond to questions that action learning team members might have to enhance clarity and specificity. Whether they stay throughout the life of the action learning team or not, they must return before the team presents its recommended solution to a decision-making body in order to review and approve the team's recommended solution. Sponsors also must be available to the team throughout the project to provide perspective and to facilitate challenges.

3. *Reframe and Agree on the Problem.* The action learning team members must ask open-ended questions of the presenter and of one another to better understand the problem and the desired goal. In the process of inquiry and reflection the team members are likely to reframe the presenting problem so it makes sense to them and to ensure that its scope and scale is within their capacity to act. Once team members agree on the reframed problem, they must gain the sponsor's acceptance. Accordingly, the team must renegotiate the problem description with its sponsor.

4. *Determine Goal.* The action learning team members consider the desired goal for which they want to develop a viable implementation or action plan. This exploration might generate one or several alternative goals. The teams must then consult with their sponsors to gain their agreement, negotiate modifications, or go back to the drawing board and repeat the process.

5. *Analyze Problem.* The problem, at this point, is to determine how to get from the current state (a problem, opportunity, or dilemma) to the desired state or goal (see Figure 11.1). The action learning team analyzes the problem situation by examining why it is important to achieve the desired state as well as why it is difficult to achieve the desired state. The team can then identify which difficulties (the various restraining forces or factors) the organization might be able to eliminate or reduce in power and, thereby, move in the direction of the desired state. Similarly, but of less significance, the team might identify ways in which the organization might increase the power and number of reasons why it is important to achieve the desired state.

6. *Generate Solution Ideas, Critique, Select.* The action learning team will create several strategies and many ideas for action steps. To test their viability, the team might engage the various subsystems and stakeholders – including sponsors and managers of team members – who are likely to be affected by the problem, its causes, and/or the implementation of a solution to gain an understanding of their reactions, needs, and preferences. This information could suggest modifications in their understanding of the context of the problem situation, the provisional goal, and/or the action steps. Since it is not realistic to expect that all involved subsystems and stakeholders will be in agreement, the team will have to negotiate political tradeoffs to select potential solutions that benefit most stakeholders and require the least number of stakeholders to sacrifice.

7. *Develop Strategies and Action Steps.* As the action learning team agrees on a particular solution, it will focus on developing a strategy that team members believe will induce members of most involved subsystems and stakeholders to support the

proposed solution. The team will then identify the specific action steps that must be taken to achieve its goal. The team should specify who would be responsible for the execution of each step, when the step should be taken, the time it is expected to take, and the resources needed to execute it effectively. The overall implementation plan should include several major milestones that, when achieved, will clearly demonstrate the project's progress. The team should present its proposed strategy and action steps to the involved subsystems and stakeholders for their reaction and feedback as a test of its viability and to gain their acceptance of the proposals. The feedback, especially critical feedback, is often extremely useful in modifying the strategy, plans, and goals.

8. *Propose Recommendations; Gain Approval; Feedback.* Each action learning team will develop a plan for presenting its recommendations to a designated authority – e.g., the advisory committee or the executive management team – for its approval, modifications, delays, or rejection. It will be up to you and other senior personnel to determine who will comprise this decision-making authority. The action learning team members must learn from their presentation of their recommended solutions. In an "after-action review," teams should learn: What went well? What could have been done better? Accordingly, the decision-making authority should be prepared to provide each action learning team with feedback describing their evaluation criteria, what they appreciated, and what they disagreed with regarding the team recommendations.

9. *Implement Action Plans.* Once the decision-making authority decides that a proposal is acceptable, it must also decide when and by whom it will be implemented. Please note that *it would be a serious error if implementation responsibilities were*

to be handed off to a team of implementers who had no involvement or participation in the creation of the strategy and plan. Implementers who did not participate as members of the action learning team will have limited emotional investment in and commitment to making the strategy and action plan work. It is not theirs. Members of the implementation team will experience the strategy and plan as being imposed upon them. A great deal of time-consuming conflict is likely to ensue. Thus, the implementation team must include as many members of the action learning team as is feasible. These team members will have invested their time and energy in crafting the goals, strategies, and plans. They will feel a sense of ownership, and they will be committed to support the implementation of the strategy and plans because they will have been part of the entire process of creating them. Further, they know the landscape and will enable information exchanges between the new implementation team members and the action learning team members, as well as between the implementation team and the various involved subsystems and stakeholders. They will have become also familiar with all involved parties and their respective interests.

10. *Monitor, Evaluate Progress and Results.* The implementation team must be oriented to the uncertainty, ambiguity, and vicissitudes of the change implementation process. The team must be prepared to assess progress toward the achievement of each major milestone, as specified in the implementation plan. As planned changes begin to be made at the primary location of the original problem situation – within a particular subsystem or the interactions between two or more related subsystems – the equilibrium of the entire system is likely to be *perturbed.* A change that takes place in the primary location is quite likely to

create secondary and tertiary changes that reverberate across interconnected, interdependent subsystems and between subsystems. Thus implementers must be alert to early indications of anticipated effects, unexpected consequences and side effects, as well as predictable surprises. While it might not be possible to predict any specific major problems that could occur as a result of implementing planned changes, team members can predict that such problems are likely to occur. Further, independent evaluation techsperts can help by designing and carrying out both quantitative and qualitative assessments of the progress and the achieved results of the planned change initiative. It is essential to have unbiased specialists to demonstrate the predicted effectiveness of the change initiative.

As you can appreciate, your role responsibilities as (one of) the organization's leaders are extensive. It will be quite difficult for you to discharge all of these responsibilities properly, effectively, and in a timely manner. You will probably choose to delegate many of these responsibilities to trusted associates. This has many benefits. It reduces your burden and shares responsibility among a number of other leaders. This can be a developmental opportunity for you and your associates. It will also demonstrate a unity of purpose among your organization's leadership. You will find it reassuring and beneficial to engage a knowledgeable personal coach or mentor to provide you with trusted advice as you make sense of the unfolding tapestry of the process of complex systems change.

CHAPTER 12.

The Commitment to Learn

As action learning teams progress in their efforts to create a proposed solution for organizational problems, there will likely emerge a tendency by some to focus more on the task and less on what has been learned from working on the task. To assure a balance between task achievement and learning, action learning coaches must persist in helping team members make explicit what they are learning.

Action learning coaches will need your explicit support. It is essential that you – visibly, and continuously – support the dual objectives of action learning. In this respect, coaches must use at least the last 20 to 30 minutes of each action learning session to debrief the team. This will help the coach maintain the balance of learning and task completion. If and when team members resist participation in the debriefing session (perhaps because they want to continue to work on the team's task or to get back to their routine jobs), coaches would remind them of their commitment to abide by the second action learning ground rule: *The coach is authorized to intervene whenever an opportunity to learn or to improve the team's performance arises.* You and other organizational leaders must support the action learning coach by publicly insisting that all team members and their respective managers must abide by the ground rules and invest their time in the debriefing process.

In this milieu, the action learning coach is obliged to systematically inquire about four levels of learning. First, the coach needs to consider *"What have team members learned about themselves?"* *"What have they learned about how their implicit assumptions influence how they think and feel and act?"* *"What have they learned about how to make their implicit assumptions explicit and then test their validity?"*

Second, the coach will assess how well each team member has done in developing the leadership and interpersonal skills they identified at the beginning of the action learning process. Team members will be obliged to say why they think they have or have not progressed in this developmental process. After each team member speaks, coaches will ask the other team members to provide the individual with feedback, i.e., what they saw and heard that leads them to believe the individual team member had or had not progressed. Third, coaches will ask each team member what she or he learned about developing high performing problem solving teams. Fourth, coaches will ask team members, *"What they have learned about how the organization deals with unprecedented change"* as well as *"What has each team member learned about how the organization's culture either enables or inhibits efforts to change"*

Action Learning and Learning Organizations. Action learning has the potential to contribute to an organization's intentional effort to become a continuously *learning organization*[4]. At a minimum, this calls for action learning teams and their members to record what they have been learning from their individual and collective experiences – from the beginning to the end of their involvement in the process. The scope of learning includes what team members recognize and embrace about acquiring leadership and interpersonal skills and knowledge,

---

4.   For additional background on learning organizations, see: Argyris & Schön, 1978, 1996; Easterby-Smith, Araujo, & Burgoyne, 1999; Marquardt, 2002; Senge, et al, 1994; and Senge, et al, 1999.

developing high performance teamwork, and knowledge and skills in intervening in intergroup and complex organizational systems change.

You or the project manager should designate staff members to develop an archival system along the lines of an in-house Wikipedia-like system so that any organizational member can enter what they have learned under a variety of relevant subject headings. Future generations of organizational members will be able to retrieve multiple entries on any recorded topic regarding what earlier team members have learned regarding how they have been affected by or involved in the action learning process. This exercise should involve the full breadth of the team learning participants including executives, champions, sponsors, stakeholders, action learning team members, implementation team members, and managers of the latter two populations.

What topic headings? What people learned during the action learning process – alone or in combination with either a leadership development program or an organizational change initiative – can be entered under topic headings that you may predetermine. For example, the chapter and section headings in this book can serve as an initial set of topic headings. Additional topic headings will emerge with continued experience or you can dedicate some staff members to combine similar learnings under new topic headings that they create.

When to enter learnings? Action learning coaches need to be consistently asking team members what they have learned at the end of each action learning session. If you decide to make the organization a learning organization, you might request or require action learning team members to briefly write and enter what they learned at regular intervals, e.g., after each session's debrief, each step of the way. You can also solicit entries from all involved internal and external stakeholders, but you will need to keep in mind that the authority to demand stakeholders' compliance might not be extant. Accordingly, you will need to find some way of helping them realize that it is in their own best interests to actively contribute to the learning organization.

Who enters the learnings into the system? It would be ideal if all involved parties – i.e., action learning team members and stakeholders – voluntarily entered what they have been learning on their own, without prompting. But that might be too much to expect. The learners will be very busy at precisely those times when it would be best to record and enter their learnings. In such circumstances, you, in concert with the champions, sponsors, and action learning coaches should consider creating a mechanism or process that makes it as easy as possible and reduces obstacles to performing this critical function. For example, you – not the action learning coach – could have sponsors request action learning teams to identify one team member (perhaps on a rotating basis) to record every team member's learning at the end of each session and enter them in the learning organization archives. A similar mechanism might be co-created with each stakeholder subsystem or group. You might also find it useful to ask the members of the advisory committee, (if there is one), and the executive management team members about what they learned throughout the process.

What is next? When the action learning, organizational change, or leadership development program is completed, you and/or the organization's executive management team should consider what, if any, additional systemic problems would be appropriate for additional action learning projects. As you consider this question, you should be attentive to the possibility that the involved parties may go through a *"decompression"* period (symptoms: relief, a desire to relax, difficulty focusing, rapidly changing focus of attention, fatigue, and irritability) that typically follows an extended period of intense involvement in dealing with a critical problem. It would be best to allow the involved parties to decompress with at least six to 10 days of *"normal"* activity before involving them in making a decision about doing it all again.

CHAPTER 13.

The Action Learning Team Coach

It is natural to be skeptical that an action learning coach can have a powerful influence in assisting a team to learn from taking action as it solves problems just by asking questions. Nonetheless, it is important that you trust the action learning process.

Trust starts with faith and is built on accumulating evidence. To start the process of building trust, you have to defer skepticism and operate on a degree of faith. In the beginning of an action learning initiative, to have faith, you will need to *understand and agree* with what action learning coaches do and why they do it. You must also understand and agree with what coaches do <u>not</u> do. With sufficient understanding, faith will sustain you until your action learning teams begin to demonstrate their effectiveness in a tangible manner. By then, trust will no longer be an issue. Toward that end, this chapter is dedicated to a detailed description of what you can expect from fully qualified action learning coaches.

The action learning coach plays a critical role in helping the team become more effective in solving complex problems and in learning how to learn from experience. As demonstrated throughout this book, the coach's role is unusual and may be confusing since it may seem similar to the role of a task or process facilitator. However, there are two major distinguishing features of the action learning coach's role functions and responsibilities. First, the coach absolutely refrains from any involvement in the content of the team's problem-solving and solution-generating activities. Second, the coach refrains from teaching team members any problem-solving methods, procedures, or mental models.

The action learning coach focuses on how and what action learning team members are learning from their participation in the team's task. The coach employs only questions to model and shape the most effective ways to ask questions, to demonstrate the power of questions to elicit useful information, to optimize team members' learning and reflection, to avoid biasing team members, and to demonstrate the links between questions, change, and impact.

The role of the action learning coach is multifaceted. The coach looks for opportunities to ask "great" questions that will help the team members learn and improve their individual and collective performance. The coach asks questions intended to encourage inquiry, reflection, and learning, questions that focus team members' attention on the team's evolutionary development, questions that heighten team members' awareness about deviations from the ground rules, and questions that help the team test and set useful team norms of acceptable behavior. In addition, the coach serves as the team's timekeeper to ensure that the team periodically discusses their learnings at the individual, team, and organizational levels and that both learning and action are accomplished at every session.

Figure 13.1. Role Functions of the Action Learning Coach

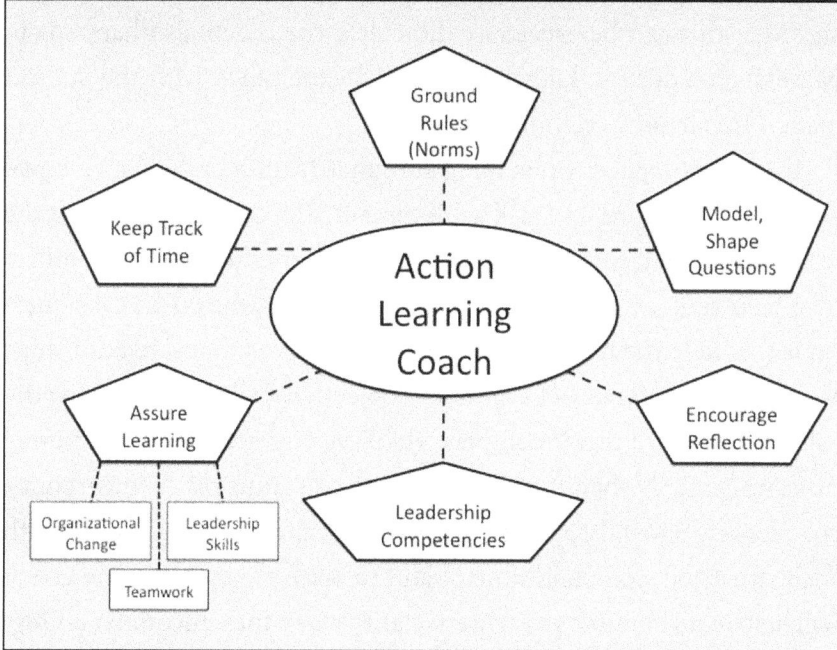

Ground Rules (Norms)

Keep Track of Time

Model, Shape Questions

Action Learning Coach

Assure Learning

Encourage Reflection

Organizational Change

Leadership Skills

Leadership Competencies

Teamwork

Action learning coaches do not get involved in creating the solution itself, but do involve themselves in the processes that team members employ in creating or finding solutions. When the team is struggling to find or create a method or procedure to help them solve the problem, coaches might ask, *"What have any of you learned – from your personal experience, workshops, or educational courses – that could help the team deal with the current difficulties?"* This usually elicits several practical "P" (programmed knowledge) memories for which, when applied, the team is grateful.

The coach does not tell the team what to do or how to do it, but does ask what the team has done well and what it could do better. Accordingly, the team members reflect upon and decide how they can improve their own performance. The coach does not make recommendations. The coach does not coach individual members. Further, the coach refrains from taking on responsibilities for performing any activity or role that team members can manage or obtain for themselves. As tempting as it might be, the coach refrains from serving as an SME; this can be especially difficult if the coach also happens to possess considerable knowledge of and experience with the subject matter; this requires self-discipline.

The coach focuses on making sure that team members give equal attention to learning and task achievement. The coach ensures that the team does not succumb to inappropriate influence from team members who have senior organizational positions; that is, the coach asks questions that help the team examine its internal hierarchical relationships and operates at a level of fairness and objectivity, while recognizing the role of feelings in team members' thinking and actions. By refraining from rescuing it when it gets into a state of confusion or uncertainty, coaches also show their confidence in the team's capacity to cope with such situations and conditions – and to learn from them. The coach will help team members to achieve clarity when they encounter ambiguous circumstances.

As a senior executive or champion, your ultimate question might be, *"How do I make sure that I am hiring a fully qualified action learning coach?"* This is a critical yet problematic question since there are no barriers that prevent unqualified persons from proclaiming themselves to be fully qualified action learning coaches. As a result, you might encounter many good-sounding *false positives* as well as *false negatives* among the true positive candidates. At issue is the existence and reputation of an independent body that certifies the competence of action learning coaches at various levels of proficiency. There is only one such body: *The World Institute for Action Learning (WIAL)* is a non-profit institute that provides education about action learning and trains and certifies action learning coaches.

Freedman and Leonard were among six pioneers who, with Mike Marquardt as the chairman, founded WIAL about eight years ago. WIAL now has trained well over a hundred certified coaches worldwide and has established affiliate institutes in many parts of the world. To learn more, check out the WIAL website at http://www.wial.org/. WIAL certifies action learning coaches at several levels: certified, professional, senior, and master. All levels go through a developmental training process; higher levels of certification are based on additional training, supervised experience, and contributions to the discipline. A list of certified coaches is accessible on the website. No other established entity certifies action learning coaches.

Still, certification alone does not guarantee that a prospective action learning coach will serve as needed. Some false positives occasionally pass through the sifting process that leads to certification. But WIAL certification is a significant beginning. Additional training beyond certification is desirable. For example, advanced training for action learning coaches through our new organization, *Learning Through Action*.

In the final analysis, it is imperative for you to pay close attention to the quality of interactions with prospective coaches when discussing the elements of a potential consulting agreement (or contract). With this book as a background, any interested leader will be able to bring up issues with prospective action learning coaches to assess their knowledge, understanding, and skills. Their responses will give a good indication of the prospects' orientation and depth of experience. From that interaction you should be able to make an intelligent, mutually beneficial, and informed selection decision.

Summary and Conclusions

We have written this book to offer you a comprehensive understanding of the action learning project process, the roles played by all involved parties, and the responsibilities that the involved parties perform. The authors, Freedman and Leonard, have conveyed this information by guiding you through a series of decisions about what kind of consultants you need or want. In addition, the book examines in detail the six essential elements of action learning and action learning projects. To repeat, they are:

1. A compelling, important, urgent, complex, unprecedented problem

2. The action learning team

3. The questioning and reflection process

4. The commitment to taking action

5. The commitment to learning

6. The action learning team coach

What you can expect from an action learning project. After this description of the action learning project process, it is important that you are clear about the value you can expect from your investment.

Again, the list of realistic expectations includes the following:

- Action learning teams can be quickly mobilized to solve unprecedented, complex, critical, urgent organizational problems.

- The knowledge and skills in participative problem solving and decision making that team members acquire are transportable to their real life routine work settings.

- The process builds powerful high performing teams that team members learn to replicate in other parts and levels of your organization.

- Action learning enables team members to learn how to learn from their work on real, critical tasks.

- The process contributes to the creation of an organizational culture that is adept at dealing effectively with change.

- Action learning contributes to the creation of your learning organization.

- Team members develop their leadership and interpersonal skills; they learn how to give and receive helpful, critical feedback.

- Team members learn to think in terms of complex, comprehensive systems.

- Team members become increasingly proficient in developing high performing teams.

- Team members gain knowledge of intergroup and organizational dynamics, including political dynamics, and skill in contributing to complex organizational systems change.

- Action learning promotes individual and collective creativity, ingenuity, and innovation.

- Team members develop networks of lasting relationships with people from other parts and levels of their organization that facilitate intergroup communication and cooperation. This has an enduring positive effect on your organization's effectiveness.

In conclusion, we want to express our hope that this book has provided the guidance you need to understand the action learning project process and that, as result, you will make intelligent, informed decisions about employing the right consultants for proper organizational purposes.

Please remember that we have made distinctions between what we think you *must* do (the essentials) in contrast with what we think you *should* do (the highly recommended). We have identified quite a number of tasks, activities, and functions that either must or should be performed. *You are ultimately responsible for making sure that the essentials are performed and that the highly recommended are seriously considered.* However, as we have mentioned previously, we do not intend to convey the expectation that you should make all the decisions or perform all of the tasks, activities, and functions personally. Rather, you should delegate many of these responsibilities to your colleagues, associates, and direct reports. This will spread the responsibilities around among a fairly large group. Performing these delegated responsibilities will be developmental activities. This will also get a large number of your organizational leaders actively involved in performing highly visible tasks, activities, and functions. Such participation generally results in increased emotional investment in and commitment to making sure that your leadership development program or your complex organizational systems change using action learning will be implemented as planned.

We stand ready to support you in these endeavors. To inquire about our availability, you can contact either of us as follows:

ARTHUR FREEDMAN, MBA, PHD
(202) 466-3921
Arthurf796@aol.com

H. SKIPTON (SKIP) LEONARD, PH.D.
(703) 437-1157
skiptonl@yahoo.com

References

Adams, M. (2009). *Change your questions, change your results.* Lambertville, NJ: Inquiry Institute.

Argyris, C., & Schön, D. (1978). *Organizational learning: A theory of action perspective,* Reading, Mass: Addison Wesley.

Argyris, C., & Schön, D. (1996) *Organizational learning II: Theory, method and practice,* Reading, Mass: Addison Wesley.

Beer, M., & Nohria, N. (2000). *Breaking the code of change.* Boston: Harvard Business School Press.

Boshyk, Y., editor (2002). *Action learning worldwide: Experiences of leadership and organizational development.* New York: Palgrave/Macmillan.

Browne, M.N., & Keeley, S.M. (2007). *Asking the right questions: A guide to critical thinking, 8th edition.* Upper Saddle River, NJ: Pearson/Prentice Hall.

Coughlan, P. & Coghlan, D. (2011). *Collaborative strategic improvement through network action learning.* Cheltenham, UK: Edward Elgar.

Dotlich, D.L., & Noel, J.L. (1998). *Action learning: How the world's top companies are re-creating their leaders and themselves.* San Francisco: Jossey-Bass.

Easterby-Smith, M., Araujo, L., & Burgoyne, J. (eds.) *Organizational learning and the learning organization*. London: Sage.

Freedman, A.M. (1997). The undiscussable sides of implementing transformational change. *Consulting Psychology Journal*, Winter, 49, 1, 51-76.

Freedman, A.M., & Zackrison, R.E. (2001). *Finding your way in the consulting jungle: A guidebook for organization development practitioners*. San Francisco: Jossey-Bass/Pfeiffer.

Freedman, A.M., & Stinson, G.H. (2004). Herding cats: Lessons learned from managing and coordinating organization development consultants. *Consulting Psychology Journal*, 56(1), 44-57.

Freedman, A.M. (2009). Working ourselves out of a job. *Organizations & Change*, 1-2.

Freedman, A.M. (2013). The application of systems theory to organizational diagnosis. In H.S. Leonard, R. Lewis, A.M. Freedman, & J. Passmore, editors, *The Wiley-Blackwell handbook of leadership, change, and organization development*. London: John Wiley & Sons.

Gasparski, W.W., & Botham, B., editors (1998). *Action learning: Praxiology: The international annual of practical philosophy and methodology, volume 6*. New Brunswick, NJ: Transaction Publishers.

Grady, V.M., Magda, B., & Grady, J.D. (2011). Organizational change, mental models, and stability: Are they mutually exclusive or inextricably linked? *Organization Development Journal*, 29, 3, 9-22.

Hackman, J.R. (2002). *Leading teams: Setting the stage for great performances*. Boston: Harvard Business School Publishing.

Hackman, J.R. (2011). *Collaborative intelligence: Using teams to solve hard problems*. San Francisco: Berrett-Khoeler.

IBM (2008). *Making change work: Continuing the enterprise of the future conversation.* IBM Institute for Business Value. Retrieved November 2, 2009, from http://935.ibm.com/services/us/gbs-making-change-work.html.

Keller, S., & Price, C. (2011). *Beyond performance: How great organizations build competitive advantage.* Hoboken, NJ: John Wiley & Sons.

Kepner, C.H., & Tregoe, B.B. (1997). *The new rational manager.* Princeton, NJ: Princeton Research Press.

Kotter, J.P. (1998). Leading change: Why transformational efforts fail. *Harvard Business Review on Change*, 1-20.

Leonard, H.S., Freedman, A.M. (2013). *Great solutions through action learning: Success every time.* Reston, VA: Learning through Action.

Mager, R.F., & Pipe, P. (1997). *Analyzing performance problems or you really oughta wanna: How to figure out why people aren't doing what they should be, and what to do about it, 3rd edition.* Atlanta, GA: The Center for Effective Performance.

Marquardt, M.J. (1999). *Action learning in action: Transforming problems and people for world-class organizational learning.* Palo Alto, CA: Davies-Black Publishing.

Marquardt, M.J. (2002). *Building the learning organization: Mastering the 5 elements for corporate learning.* Palo Alto, CA: Davies-Black Publications.

Marquardt, M.J., Leonard, H.S., Freedman, A.M., & Hill, C.C. (2009). *Action learning for developing leaders and organizations: Principles, strategies, and cases.* Washington, D.C.: American Psychological Association.

Marquardt, M.J. (2011). *Optimizing the power of action learning: Real-time strategies for developing leaders, building teams, and transforming organizations, 2nd edition.* Boston: Nicholas Brealey Publishing.

O'Neil, J., & Marsick, V.J. (2007). *Understanding action learning: Theory into practice.* New York: American Management Association.

Revans, R. (1998). *ABC of action learning: Empowering managers to act and to learn from action.* London: Lemos & Crane.

Rothwell, W.J. (1999). *The action learning guidebook: A real-time strategy for problem solving, training design, and employee development.* San Francisco: Jossey-Bass/Pfeiffer.

Schwarz, R. (2002). *The skilled facilitator: A comprehensive resource for consultants, facilitators, managers, trainers, and coaches, 2nd edition.* San Francisco: Jossey-Bass.

Senge, P. et al. (1994) *The fifth discipline fieldbook: Strategies and tools for building a learning organization.* New York: Doubleday/Currency.

Senge, P. et al (1999) *The dance of change: The challenges of sustaining momentum in learning organizations,* New York: Doubleday/Currency).

Smith, M.E. (2002). Success rates for different types of organizational change. *Performance Improvement,* Wiley Online Library.

Standish Group International (2009). *CHAOS summary 2009.* Retrieved November 1, 2009 from http://standishgroup.com/newsroom/chaos_2009.php.

Strebel, P. (1998). Why do employees resist change. *Harvard Business Review on Change,* 139-157.

Torbert, B., & associates (2004). *Action inquiry: The secret of timely and transforming leadership.* San Francisco: Berrett-Koehler.

Ulrich, D., Kerr, S., & Ashkenas, R. (2002). *The GE workout: How to implement GE's revolutionary method for busting bureaucracy and attacking organizational problems – fast!* New York: McGraw-Hill.

Vogt, E.E., Brown, J., & Issacs, D. (2003). *The art of powerful questions.* Mill Valley, CA: Whole Systems Associates

About the Authors

Arthur M. Freedman, MBA, Ph.D. is a licensed consulting organizational psychologist who specializes in action learning team coaching, executive coaching, leadership development, developing high performing teams, organization development, and planning and implementing complex organizational change. He is a Co-Founder of the *World Institute of Action Learning(WIAL)*. He has consulted throughout the world to public and private sector organizations (e.g., USA, Dubai, Lithuania, Vietnam, Singapore, USSR/Russia, Sweden, Zimbabwe, South Africa, England, and Germany). He is an adjunct Professor at the *Carey Business School, Johns Hopkins University,* and a Visiting Scholar, *Center for Organizational Dynamics, University of Pennsylvania.*

He received many awards over the years: *1994 RHR International Award for Excellence in Consulting Psychology;* the 1997 *Elliott Jaques Award* for the outstanding *Consulting Psychology Journal* article ("Pathways and Crossroads to Institutional Leadership"), the *2007 Harry and Miriam Levinson Award for Exceptional Contributions to Organizational Consulting Psychology;* the 2011 *Hall of Fame Award* from the National Hispanic Institute; and the *2012 Distinguished*

Psychologist in Management award from the Society of Psychologists in Management.

He has spoken at more than 115 conferences worldwide, and has over 120 publications including books, book chapters, and journal articles. Among his most recent publications are: "Action learning in multicultural contexts," (2011) *Intercultural Management Quarterly*; "Using action learning for organization development and change" (2011), *OD Practitioner; and* "Some implications of validation of the leadership pipeline concept: Guidelines for assisting managers-in-transition," (2011) *The Psychologist-Manager Journal.* "Executive consultation under pressure: A case study" co-authored with James Perry, (2010) *Consulting Psychology Journal; Action Learning for developing leaders and organizations,* co-authored with Michael Marquardt, Skipton Leonard, and Cori Hill (2009, American Psychological Association); *Consulting Psychology: Selected papers of Harry Levinson,* co-edited with Ken Bradt (2008, American Psychological Association); "Swimming upstream: The challenge of managing promotions" (2005) in *Filling the leadership pipeline,* Rob Kaiser, editor (2005, Center for Creative Leadership); "Action research: Origins and applications for OD&C practitioners" (2006) in *The NTL handbook of organization development and change;* "The role of psychologists in the U.S. Intelligence Community," (2008) *Consulting Psychology Journal.*

Skipton Leonard, Ph.D.

Trained as a social and organizational psychologist, Dr. Skipton (Skip) Leonard was a co-founder of the World Institute for Action Learning (WIAL) in 2006. Skip is currently Principal and Managing Director for Learning Thru Action, LLC, a consulting firm that provides action-based solutions for developing organizations and people. Prior to helping found WIAL, Dr. Leonard was a Vice President and Executive Consultant with Personnel Decisions International (PDI). Over the years, Skip has consulted with numerous Fortune 500 and Global 1000 companies such as Microsoft, Target, AMA-China, Wells Fargo, American Express, AstraZeneca, Boeing, Bechtel, Daimler Chrysler, Dell, NCS-Pearson, and SAIC. He also has consulting experience with NGO's such as the IMF and World Bank as well as US government organizations such as National Institutes of Health, The Department of Commerce, the Army, the Postal Service, General Services Administration, Department of Agriculture, Defense Intelligence Agency, and General Accounting Office.

Dr. Leonard has been a faculty member at a number of top universities including the Carey School of Business at Johns Hopkins University, the Department of Human and Organizational Learning at the George Washington University, the School of Public Affairs at American University, the graduate department of Psychology at George Mason University, and the State University of New York at Plattsburgh.

Dr. Leonard received his doctoral and undergraduate degrees in Psychology from New York University and Middlebury College respectively. He is a licensed psychologist in the state of Virginia and served his country as an officer in the US Army.

A leader in his profession, Dr. Leonard is a Member of the American Psychological Association and Past-President and Fellow of the Society of Consulting Psychology. He was also the founding editor of the peer-reviewed journal, Consulting Psychology Journal.

Over the years, Dr. Leonard has received many awards including the Chairman's Award for Innovation (PDI), The Founders Award by NYU, and a special commendation for leadership and commitment to the Society of Consulting Psychology. He is also Executive Board Member Emeritus for the World Institute for Action Learning.

Dr. Leonard has over 75 books, book chapters, articles, and professional presentations to his credit including:

Leonard, H.S., Lewis, R., Freedman, A.M. & Passmore. J. (Eds.) (2013). The *Wiley-Blackwell Handbook of the Psychology of Leadership, Change & OD*. Chichester, UK: Wiley-Blackwell.

Leonard, H.S., & Freedman, A.M. (2013). Learning Thru Action.

Marquardt, M., Leonard, H.S., Freedman, A.M., Hill, C. (2009). *Action learning for developing leaders and organizations: principles, strategies, and cases. Washington:* American Psychological Association Press.

Hill, C., Leonard, H.S., and Sokol, M. (2006). *Action learning guide: real learning, real results.* Minneapolis: Personnel Decisions International Press.

www.ingramcontent.com/pod-product-compliance
Lightning Source LLC
Chambersburg PA
CBHW062035200326
41519CB00017B/5040